The T[Guide To Health And Happiness

101 Nutrition and Lifestyle Secrets

By Timothy Baumann, CHC

Published by Wellness For Life Network, LLC
Ogden, Utah 84403

Visit our website at www.depressiontohappiness.com

10 9 8 7 6 5 4 3 2 1

Cover design by Timothy Baumann

ISBN: 978-0-9976187-3-0

Dedication

This book is dedicated to my pre-teen and teenage granddaughters, Mekiella, Angelina and Gracie who helped me write this book.

You are the oldest of 11 grandchildren.
As children affected by divorce you are an inspiration to all. You have and are currently enduring some hardships due to fathers who suffer from addictions. In one case a father has a history of being in and out of jail.

But know this, you are not alone. There are thousands of other teenagers in similar situations.

This book is also dedicated to all those other teenagers who are looking for health and happiness. It is my hope and prayer that you ALL will find the Pathway to Happiness and enjoy - The Happiness Journey.

DISCLAIMER

None of the information contained within this book has been approved by the Food and Drug Administration. Also consult with your health professional before you change your eating habits or embarking on a new exercise routine. This book makes no claims to diagnose or cure any mental or physical maladies. We make no claims to any outcomes nor guarantee specific results.

Published by Wellness For Life Network, LLC
Ogden, Utah 84403

ACKNOWLEDGEMENTS

I need to acknowledge the Institute of Integrated Nutrition (IIN) and its founder Joshua Rosenthal. It was there that I learned about health, wellness and about Primary Foods and Secondary Foods.

Primary Foods are foods that you do not eat but are essential for good health and Secondary Foods are the foods that you do eat. Both Foods have to be in balance for great health.

You must have an ample supply of both Secondary Foods and healthy Primary Foods to have good health and an abundance of happiness. Life is such a drag without one or the other. My education helped me develop my skills as a certified health coach so I can help others find and develop health and happiness. Thanks again to IIN.

TABLE OF CONTENTS

PREFACE

"The Teenagers Guide To Health And Happiness – 101 Nutrition and Lifestyle Secrets" is a revised version for teenagers that came from 101 Nutrition And Lifestyle Secrets For Health And Happiness. Both books are a very condensed versions of a complete holistic program that I put together to help individuals who suffer from symptom of depression and anxiety. It is called *Depression To Happiness – The 100 Day Challenge*. (More information can be found at www.depressiontohappiness.com/the100daychallenge)

I was motivated to write The 100 Day Challenge because of my wife and some of her family members.

A number of years ago my mother-in-law committed suicide and a few years later my brother-in-law committed suicide. Well luck would have it, my wife became depressed. I knew I had to do something or she might be the next one in her family to commit suicide.

I wrote this book because of the struggles my grandchildren are going through as they are entering their teenage years. Both sets of parents went through a divorce with one father who is always in and out of jail because of an addiction to drugs and alcohol and the other father who abuses alcohol.

I know that they are not alone in their struggles, as tens of thousands of teenagers are struggling with life. All have their stories but all deserve to have great health and abundance of happiness.

I went to nutrition school for a year and then spent two years researching for natural, holistic ways to dealing with depression symptoms. This book will help deal and overcome depression and anxiety and at the same time help anyone gain better health and more happiness. These tips and secrets will help everyone.

The Teenagers Guide To Health And Happiness – 101 Nutrition and Lifestyle Secrets is a collection of all the different tips, secrets and action items that can and will help bring more health and happiness into your life and diminish or eliminate depression and anxiety symptoms. You get a little information on each secret and an action item.

The purpose of this book is to help you improve your overall health by giving you simple ideas and action steps to do. When your body is given the right nutrition, your body and brain will be healthy and will function properly. When it comes down to it, most all diseases and mood disorders can be improved or eliminated with proper nutrition and lifestyle changes. Try these 101 secrets and you will find the journey to peace and happiness quite enjoyable.

The secret to success is in the action items. The idea is to read the book all the way through. Then each week work on implementing each action item and making that tip part of your daily life. Each action item is simple and easy to implement. Please don't knock any of the tips. They work and I challenge you to try each one. The proof is in the pudding.

Health and Happiness is all about the journey, not the destination.

INTRODUCTION

THE HAPPINESS JOURNEY

"For a long time it seemed to me that life was about to begin - real life. But there was always some obstacle in the way, something to be gotten through first, some unfinished business, time to still be served, a debt to be paid.

"Then life would begin. At last it dawned on me that these obstacles were my life.

"This perspective has helped me to see that there is <u>no way TO</u> happiness. Happiness <u>IS the way</u>.

So, treasure every moment that you have. And treasure it more because you shared it with someone special, special enough to spend your time and remember that time waits for no one.

So stop waiting
until you finish school,
until you go back to school,
until you lose ten pounds,
until you gain ten pounds,
until you have kids,
until your kids leave the house,
until you start work,

until you retire,

until you get married,

until you get divorced,

until Friday night,

until Sunday morning,

until you get a new car or home,

until your car or home is paid off,

until spring,

until summer,

until fall,

until winter,

until you are off welfare,

until the first or fifteenth,

until your song comes on,

until you've had a drink,

until you've sobered up,

until you die,

until you are born again

to decide that there is no better time than

right now to be happy.

Happiness is a journey, not a destination.
--Alfred D. Souza

Health and Happiness is the pursuit of most teenagers in the world today. Unfortunately many teens cannot find this allusive feeling. Why can't many teens find real happiness along with health? Here is something to think about –

> *INSANITY:* Doing the same thing over and over and expecting a different result.
>
> *SADNESS:* Staying on the same lifestyle path and expecting happiness.
>
> *HAPPINESS:* The Happiness Journey may require you to change paths by making lifestyle changes.

So if you want to enjoy the fruits of the happiness journey you must make some changes. To make these changes do not require taking giant steps. It's just the opposite. You only need to make consistent, small, and daily changes. If you do, one day soon you will find that you are on a different path, one that I call the happiness journey.

The body, mind and soul (spirit) must have all the proper nutrients to obtain and maintain good health. When your body feels good it is so much easier to be happy. These nutrients are found in two main food groups – **Primary Foods** and **Secondary Foods**.

- *PRIMARY FOODS*: Keep in mind that not all nutrients come from the food we eat. Primary foods are foods that we do not eat. These are also considered Lifestyle Choices. They following fall into these categories – **Exercise, Careers, Relationships, and Spirituality**. If any of these areas in your life are missing or they are weak, you are not going to be getting the nutrition you need for health and happiness. Weakness in any of these 4 areas will cause you stress instead of strength.

- **SECONDARY FOODS:** These foods are the ones you do eat and drink. These are foods that provide most of the different nutrients that your body needs to grow and maintain good health. They provide nutrients such as Vitamins, Minerals, Micro and Macro Nutrients, Proteins, Carbohydrates, etc. Without adequate levels of all these different nutrients your body and mind will suffer.

This book is a list of 101 secret tips to incorporate into your daily life to help you to improve your physical health, your mental health and your spiritual or soul's health.

Keep in mind this book is **NOT** an exhaustive study of each tip. They are just that, tips to plant healthy seeds in your mind. It is up to you to fully research each topic. Most all of these tips will apply to you at some time during your teenage years.

I cannot guarantee results. But I can tell you one thing. Those individuals, who put forth the effort to apply as many of these tips into their lives as possible, will see some great results.

I am not diagnosing nor giving medical advice, nor do I promote these tips as a cure for any mental or physical disease. But I will tell you that these tips have helped many people with mood disorders such as depression and anxiety, deal with illnesses and diseases. They have helped people with physical and spiritual disorders.

I also want you to know that there have been studies done on most all of these tips so there is sound scientific backing for these tips. You will find that this is true if you will do a little research.

Again, this is not an in-depth study on each tip, but you are given enough information to develop an understanding of the importance of the tip in your diet and lifestyle.

As part of each tip there is an action item. <u>The real secret is in doing the action items.</u> The evidence is in the results. In other words, do the action items and you will see and feel the results.

Baseline Evaluation

Now before you get started you need to first set a baseline for each of the major areas in your young life. You need to really know where you need to focus most of your time and energy. So to do this you will need to go to the resource section at the end of the book and copy the "Bicycle Of Life" which is my version of the "Wheel of Life".

LIFE: PRIMARY WHEEL   **HEALTH: SECONDARY WHEEL**

Instructions:

For each section on each wheel, you need to ask yourself, **'How satisfied am I with how things are going with section** _____

in my life?' The outer rim of the tire is a 10 and the hub (center) of the wheel is a 0.

Place a dot along the line (spoke) where you are in each category. When it comes to the Stress Management there are two sections, one on each wheel. I want you to think about stress as it relates to the other areas of that particular wheel, not as a whole. On the Primary Wheel think about stress as it relates to your relationships, career, your spirituality or the other sections of that wheel.

With the Secondary Wheel, evaluate your stress when it comes to your health, weight, mind and body, etc. Now take a look at your stress ratings for each wheel. You may find that most of your stress is related to your primary foods or maybe it is with your health. You may also find that whichever wheel has the lowest satisfaction rating for stress will also have some of the lowest ratings in some of the other sections. This may indicate which areas are causing you the most stress and therefore needs the most work. Now connect all the dots.

LIFE: PRIMARY WHEEL　　　**HEALTH: SECONDARY WHEEL**

How round are your two wheels?　How smooth is your ride in life?

Keep one thing in mind. We are looking for smooth wheels NOT perfect 10's in each area. You will have the rest of your life to make each area a 10!

This will now be your baseline. At the end of the 101 steps you will repeat the process to see just how far you have traveled on your Happiness Journey.

Before you make any major changes in your diet or include exercise to your daily routine, please consult with a medical professional.

Enjoy the tips and enjoy the journey to better health and happiness!

PART 1 - PRIMARY FOODS

"Food is more than what you find on your plate. Healthy relationships, regular physical activity, a fulfilling career and a spiritual practice can fill your soul and satisfy your hunger for life. When primary food is balanced and satiated, your life feeds you, making what you eat secondary".

The Founder of Institute of Integrative Nutrition, Joshua Rosenthal

Joshua Rosenthal also said, *"We hunger for play, touch, romance, intimacy, love, achievement, success, art, music, self-expression, leadership, excitement, adventure and spirituality. All of these elements are essential forms of nourishment. The extent to which we are able to incorporate them determines how enjoyable and worthwhile our lives feel."*

SECRET #1 – SET HEALTH GOALS – 8-7-2-1-0

Everyone needs to have goals in their lives, even teenagers. This is especially true when it comes to your health. Since there are so many different diets and ideas on how to have a healthy life I have found a system to help remember 5 simple health goals.

Can you remember 8-7-2-1-0? If you can remember these numbers with their associated health goal you will be able to improve your physical and mental health. By all means if you don't like these goals create your own, but create and write down your goals.

Get 8 Hours Of Sleep EVERY Night

- Getting enough sleep every night is so important to your mental and physical health that 2 secrets have been devoted to sleep.
- Sleep is when the body and brain have a chance to detoxify and repair.

Eat 7 Servings of Fruits and Vegetables Daily (5 Veggies and 2 Fruits)

- Concentrate on getting enough vegetables as it is easy to get enough fruit.
- Add veggies to your breakfast menu, grab some veggies for a snack, and add a nice green or vegetable salad to your meal. Be creative if you have to, just get the veggies into your diet.

2 Hours Or Less Of Screen Time

- Screen Time includes TV, computer, cellphones, etc. unless it is strictly for homework. Reduce social media time.
- Get outdoors and do fun activities with family and friends.
- Have face-to-conversations with other people. Read a book.

Participate In 1 Hour Of Physical Activity

- 30 Minutes of meaningful exercise. Aerobic, Strength Training, Hiking, Running, Walks etc.
- 30 Minutes of physical activities. Take the stairs instead of the elevator, park on the other side of the parking lot and walk. These are just a couple of ideas. Be creative and have fun!

Drink 0 (Zero) Soft Drinks (Soda), Juices, Energy Drinks, Coffee, Tea or Alcohol

- Drink More WATER! Replace all these sugary caffeinated drinks with pure clean water.

- If you can tolerate it drink more milk, especially whole milk. (HINT: Eating Healthy Fats Do Not Make You Fat)
- If you can't give it all up at once then just start replacing one drink a day for a week then replace another and so on until you are off the sugar and caffeine.

ACTION ITEM: Starting <u>Today</u> implementing the 8-7-2-1-0 healthy goal and health system. OR write your own health goals and the steps to achieve them.

SECRET #2 - POSITIVE SELF TALK

Self-talk is that conversation that goes on within your mind and your inner self. It is that inner voice in your mind that says stuff that you don't necessarily say out loud. Sometimes this self-talk happens and you don't even realize it going on. It can be a quiet discussion going on in the background of your mind. Just know that what you say in your mind <u>does</u> determine a lot about how you feel about yourself and who you ultimately become.

Self-talk is not just random thoughts, day-dreaming or chatter in your mind. Self-talk creates reality. If you keep telling yourself that you can do something then it probably will happen. On the other hand, if you keep telling yourself that you can't accomplish something then you are probably right.

How you see and relate to yourself is determined by your self-talk. It also may determine how others see you or how you present yourself in other people's eyes. Your self-esteem and confidence level is greatly impacted by your self-talk.

Both positive and negative self-talk have a huge influence on how you feel. It is the negative self-talk that will cause the most damage. We are all our own worst critics and we just love to push the replay button and replay the negative events or shortcomings over and over. The more attention you give to these negative thoughts the harder it is to put them behind you.

Happy people, including teenagers, seem to be able to put those occasional bad days behind them. According to a survey of 231 college students, all those with an <u>overall positive outlook on life</u> were the ones who were more likely to look back on a negative event and realize how much better things are for them today, plus, they are able to see what was learned from that experience.

You can talk yourself into a serious case of depression, anxiety or other mood disorder. Depression can be the outcome, unless you can get control of most of your negative self-talk. Research has found that those individuals who have clinical depression also have frequent and persistent destructive self-talk.

It can be difficult to turn **'Off'** the negative self-talk. To do so you must have a plan or a simple system. Here are a few tips on how to turn off the negative self-talk.

- *Distance Yourself.* No matter how strong willed you think you are, you can't expel negative talk forever just using will power. You can however step back away from it for a bit by thinking about your 'Happy Thought'. (Secret #4)
- *Distract Yourself.* It is hard to have a conversion with yourself when involved in an activity. Try doing an activity that will fully engage your mind like a crossword puzzle, playing basketball, or working on your favorite hobby.
- *Save Those Thoughts For Later.* You can set some time aside later in the day or just before bedtime for this

negative conversation with yourself. Chances are pretty good that when that time comes those negative thoughts will be gone or not be as strong.

- **Rebuke Them.** You can just demand that they leave because you do not believe they are true. When you do, your negative thoughts could just dissolve and go away.

Here are some tips on how to turn **'On'** the positive self-talk when you need it. These are needed right after you rebuke or distract the negative self-talk. You must have a plan to turn on the positive talk.

- **Pay Attention To Your Self-talk.** Start paying closer attention and really listen to what you are saying to yourself. This will help you realize when you need to change the direction of your conversation and start with the positive self-talk.
- **Practice Positive Self-talk.** Like everything else in life, you have to practice if you want to become good at something. So practice, practice and practice some more.
- **Have Positive Thoughts In Reserve.** Memorize a few positive thoughts, quotes or statements and have them ready to use when you catch yourself having a negative self-talk session. You just keep saying the positive thought over and over until you drown out the negative side of the conversion.

You must master the art of positive self-talk so that you can have good health, both physically and mentally. You can master the skill by learning more about self-talk and then practicing positive self-talk every day. Your body, mind and spirit will love you for it.

Action Item: Pay more attention to your self-talk conversations. Try one or more tips to change or end any negative self-talk conversations.

SECRET #3 - AS A MAN THINKETH

"For As A Man Thinketh In His Heart, So Is He." Proverbs 23:7

In other words – Your Thoughts control your actions and who you become!

This simple idea is one of the most powerful concepts known to man, but it is not fully understood nor practiced by many. It applies to all areas of your life. Your thoughts can literally decide what happens in your life. If you can control your thoughts, you control your circumstances, successes and your entire life.

An English gentleman by the name of James Allen wrote a book, **"As A Man Thinketh,"** that was published in 1901. He understood the importance of and the influence that your thoughts have on your personal life.

Here are a few thoughts from his book:

"A man is literally *what he thinks*, his character being the complete sum of all his thoughts."

"Man is made or unmade by himself; in the armory of thought he forges the weapons by which he destroys himself; he also fashions the tools with which he builds for himself heavenly mansions of joy and strength and peace."

"Every thought-seed sown or allowed to fall into the mind, and to take root there, produces its own, blossoming sooner or later into act, and bearing its own fruitage of opportunity and circumstances. Good thoughts bear good fruit, bad thoughts bad fruit."

"Not what he wishes and prays for does a man get, but what he justly earns. His wishes and prayers are only gratified and answered when they harmonize with his thoughts and actions."

"Disease and health, like circumstances, are rooted in thought."

"Until thought is linked with purpose there is no intelligent accomplishment."

"As the physically weak man can make himself strong by careful and patient training, so the man of weak thoughts can make them strong by exercising himself in right thoughts."

"A man can only rise, conquer, and achieve by lifting up his thoughts."

"Dream lofty dreams, and as you dream, so shall you become."

As you can see James Allen was a very thoughtful and insightful individual that has provided you and I with some serious things to think about. Change Your Thoughts – Change Your Life!

*Action item: Read and Study "As A Man Thinketh" by James Allen Reading time is about an hour or so. **OR** Read and really think about the above quotes. Discuss them with your parents or trusted friend. It will be a life changing experience.*

SECRET #4 - AFFIRMATIONS –
Reprogramming The Mind

af·firm·a·tion   ˌafərˈmāSH(ə)n/ *Noun*

1. The action or process of affirming something or being affirmed.
   Synonyms: declaration, statement, proclamation, pronouncement

2. Emotional support or encouragement.

From time to time we all have a problem with negative self-talk. Since this is true, you will need to implement methods to help reprogram your mind towards positive self-talk and thoughts.

Affirmations are one simple way to help reprogram your thoughts and provide yourself emotional support and encouragement.

Affirmations are generally short, concise, powerful and especially positive statements. These statements describe a desired goal or situation, and the statement is repeated often throughout the day until it is imbedded into the subconscious mind.

When the statement or statements are repeated over and over your subconscious mind will start to work on your behalf to make the positive statement become a reality. Your subconscious mind will accept the statements as the truth or reality whether you say it to yourself or out loud. It will attract events or situations into your life that will help your statements come true. So it is important that only positive statements be used in affirmations in order to get the positive results you desire.

Tips on how to write and do affirmations:

1. Keep the affirmations short and not too long.
2. Use positive words with no negative undertones or references. Use a statement like "I am losing weight" instead of "I am not fat". Which statement brings positive images to your mind? The words you use have to bring a positive mental image of what you want.
3. Write the statements using the present tense such as, "I am totally relaxed and stress free", instead of "I will be totally relaxed and stress free". Can you feel and see the difference? The subconscious mind will work overtime to make a present statement happen now.
4. REPEAT these statements as often as possible throughout the day. Do not affirm while driving or any other activity that requires your full attention. You can try to set 5-10 minutes aside for special affirmation sessions several times a day. Repeat out loud when you are alone. Read them, think about them, and visualize the statements.
5. RELAX as much as possible when going over your affirmations. A relaxed body helps relax the mind.
6. FOCUS your full attention on each of the words that make up your affirmation.
7. FAITH in what you are sayings and having a strong Desire will bring faster results.
8. SEE and FEEL what you want to be true in your life. Then regardless of your current situation your subconscious mind will attract your affirmation into your life.

Feel free to use any of the following examples of some simple affirmations. If you would like you can modify them to match your personal desires or just use them the way they are.

Simple Affirmations:

- I have a lot of energy.
- My body is healthy and functioning in a very good way.
- I am calm and relaxed in every situation.
- I study and comprehend fast.
- I am living in the house of my dreams.
- I radiate love and happiness.
- My thoughts are under my control.
- I have a good and loving relationship with my wife/husband/child.
- I am successful in whatever I do.
- I have a wonderful and satisfying job.
- Everything is getting better and better every day.

More Complex Affirmations

- My thoughts are filled with positivity and my life is plentiful with prosperity.
- My efforts are being supported by the universe; my dreams manifest into reality before my eyes.
- My obstacles are moving out of my way; my path is pointed toward greatness.
- I am at peace with all that has happened, is happening now, and that will happen.
- I forgive those who have harmed me in my past and peacefully remove them and move on.
- Happiness is a choice. I base my happiness on my own accomplishments and the blessings I have been given.

Action item: Find or write 2 affirmations. Review and repeat these affirmations multiple times a day for 1 week.

SECRET #5 - THE PETER PAN SOLUTION –
Happy Thoughts

You may or may not remember the movie - 'HOOK'. This movie is about Peter Pan as an adult. (Played by the late Robin Williams) He forgets that he is THE Peter Pan from the storybook.

Captain Hook kidnaps Peter Pans 2 children and takes them back to 'Never Never Land' to make them pirates. As an adult Peter Pan had forgotten about Never, Never Land and how to fly.

In order to fight Captain Hook and to rescue his children from the pirates, Peter had to learn how to fly again. Tinker Bell knew the secret and told Peter Pan that he could not fly until he found and thought about his **"HAPPY THOUGHT"**. Once he figured out his happy thought Peter Pan could fly. Hs happy thought was the birth of his first child, his son.

You must find **YOUR** – 'Happy Thought'. Your happy thought(s) can be about anything you want. The best happy thoughts are from a positive experience you've had sometime in your life.

Think about this experience now. Try to remember how it felt. Remember the smells, the touch, the sounds, the taste and the feelings in your heart. Make the thought as real as possible. Try to re-live the moment in your mind.

How did that make you feel? Did this memory put a smile on your face? Did the current feelings of sadness or worry start to diminish?

Once you really get your Happy Thought down, use it daily when thoughts of sadness or worry start to plague your mind and watch those negative feeling melt away.

You will not be able to fly, but your spirit will.

Action item: Remember and develop 2-3 "Happy Thoughts" and file them away in your mind for use on those sad or worry days.

SECRET #6 - SLEEP – A Time For Renewal

Did you know that during deep sleep your body renews itself by repairing muscles and tissues as well as build up your energy supplies for the next day? This is also the time when your body undergoes a detox – the body rids itself of toxins from all the different systems.

Teenagers need between 8 to 9 hours of sleep **every** night in order to maintain good health. This may be impossible for some people. But know that consistency is the key and cutting back on sleep can have more harmful effects than you know.

According to all the medical literature, based on huge amounts of studies, lack of sleep can have the following NEGATIVE effects:

- Increased risk of depression, anxiety and other mood disorders
- High blood pressure and other heart related diseases
- Obesity
- Brain fog and short term memory loss.
- Promotes poor decisions

This is just a short list of some of the negative effects a lack of sleep has on the body and mind.

During sleep the brain undergoes a process called *'memory-consolidation'*. This process is when the brain takes all the new information learned during the day and places it into the memory banks – short term and long term storage.

The brain also uses this time to replenish the supply of different neurotransmitters such as dopamine and serotonin – which help elevate your mood during the day.

Studies now show that all cells and body systems in your body greatly benefit from getting enough sleep. The best thing you can do for your brain, body and also your mind is to get 8-9 hours of sleep. Getting enough sleep is a great way to take care of your body, mind and spirit.

ACTION ITEM: Calculate backwards and figure out what time you have to be in bed each night in order to get 8 hours of sleep. Write it down and work hard to be in bed on time, no matter what. Your health depends on it.

SECRET #7 – SLEEP: How To Get 8 to 9 Hours

Do you want a healthy and happy life?

If so you must get 8 hours of good quality and continuous sleep. This will give your body the rest it needs and a chance to unwind and to detox itself.

Here are some tips to help get more quality sleep. These tips are Simple and Easy but you will have to make some lifestyle changes.

This is the time, during your teenage years, to develop good sleep habits that will carry with you throughout the rest of your life.

1. Develop and maintain a routine schedule at night. Go to bed at the same time every night and get up at the same time every morning. Do this even on the weekends. It helps set and maintain your body-clock rhythms.
2. Do not use electronics the hour before bed. This includes TV, cellphone, gaming devices, etc. The artificial light has been shown, in studies, to stimulate the brain and therefore making it harder to fall asleep.
3. Avoid eating large meals 2 hours before going to bed.
4. Avoid drinking caffeine 8 hours before going to bed. Studies show caffeine stays in your body up to 8 hours and makes falling and staying asleep more difficult.
5. Make your bedroom totally dark. Turn off all the lights and put up blackout curtains (like those used in most hotels).
6. Try doing some deep breathing exercises, meditation or listening to soft relaxing music before going to sleep. I love listening to guided-visualization CD's.

Try some of these different tips to help get good quality sleep. For a healthy, happy and energetic life you MUST find ways to get 8 hours of quality sleep every night.

ACTION ITEM: This week try one of the above suggestions and see if you don't sleep better and longer. Settle for nothing less than 8 hours of sleep a night.

SECRET #8 – HOME DETOX – Personal Care And Cleaners

DETOX - *a process in which one abstains from or rids the body of toxic or unhealthy substances; detoxification.*

You may not only need to detox the body (which we will discuss in a later secret) you may need to detox or remove harmful chemicals from your personal care products and household cleaners. This is an important way to keep your body away from these harmful chemicals.

These toxins can get into your body by breathing, or through the skin. Some chemicals can mess up your biochemistry and affect your health down to the cellular level.

These chemicals are called endocrine disrupters. Just remember that they 'disrupt' the hormones in the body including the ones that keep your metabolism (digestion) running right.

It is not enough to cut down on chemically loaded process foods. You really need to remove harmful toxins from your HOME. These chemicals can be found in cleaning products, make-up, and personal care products.

These can be swapped out with products that are more natural based and better for your health and the environmet. Here are the first three areas to start with:

- Make-Up, Personal Care and Beauty Supplies such as shampoo, deodorant, toothpaste, mouthwash, etc. These are a major source of 'chemicals' that can be toxic to your body. You can find such toxins as lead, mercury, toluene, parabens, formaldehyde, and phthalates, just to name a few. There are more and more 'all natural' brands of make-up and personal care lines on the market.

- Household Cleaners – These chemical-based cleaners are exposing you to many harsh and poisonous substances. Some of the worst ones are the drain cleaners, oven cleaners and toilet bowl cleaners. You can easily change to all Natural Cleaners such as white vinegar, castile soap, lemon juice, baking soda, etc. Sometimes just plain water will clean something good enough. There are also a lot of companies that are starting to market 'environmentally' friendly cleaners and soaps.
- Another common source of toxins in the home is artificial room deodorizers! These spray product contain VOC's (volatile organic compounds) that are sprayed into the air you breathe. These VOCs can cause drowsiness, headaches, nausea, and dizziness and can impair memory and moods. Use natural products like essential oils to freshen up your rooms.

These are just a few of the places you can start to detox your home. Talk with your parents and educate them and work together to rid your home of these toxic chemicals. Your body, brain will feel great and your moods will soar once you detox your home and your body. Make it a priority to detox your home first and then detox your body. Your overall health will improve.

ACTION ITEM: This week find two toxic products in your home and replace them with a non-toxic version. Then the following week replace another and then another.

RELATIONSHIPS

SECRET #9 - THE GOLDEN RULE – How To Treat People, Including Yourself

> *"Do unto others as you would have them do unto you."*
> Bible

This rule seems like a simple way to live a person's life, but look around you. There are daily examples in the news where people are NOT treating others the way they would like to be treated. Some people seem to believe the opposite is the better way to live – 'Do unto others <u>before</u> they do it unto you.' This is why they will scam you, steal from you and maybe hurt you, before someone does it to them. This is a sad way to live life.

The idea of treating other the way you want to be treated is not just a Christian based rule of life. Similar rules can be found in most all religions, for example;

Buddhism	*Hurt not others in ways that you yourself would find hurtful.* Udana-Varga 5,1
Hinduism	*This is the sum of duty; do naught onto others what you would not have them do unto you.* Mahabharata 5,1517
Islam	*No one of you is a believer until he desires for his brother that which he desires for himself.* Sunnah

Judaism	*What is hateful to you, do not do to your fellowman. This is the entire Law; all the rest is commentary.*
	Talmud, Shabbat 3rd
Taoism	*Regard your neighbor's gain as your gain, and your neighbor's loss as your own loss.*
	Tai Shang Kan Yin P'ien

As you can see they all teach essentially the same principle. As you put this idea into practice, you will also find that others will treat you better.

Now here is a new twist to this idea. The golden rule applies to you and how you need to treat yourself.

"Treat yourself the way you would want others to treat you."

Not everyone is going to treat you well, so at the very minimum you need to treat yourself well. Sometimes this is hard to do. It seems easy to treat others well while neglecting or even being hurtful to yourself. It takes a concentrated effort to make sure you are treating yourself well while you treating others nice.

You are special! Let me repeat that – YOU ARE SPECIAL, <u>so treat yourself special</u> while you are treating everyone else special. If you treat you AND others special, most everyone else will start treating you special in return. It works.

Action item: This week apply the Golden Rule to yourself and others. Most importantly, treat yourself like you would like others to treat you.

SECRET #10 - HUGS – Give Them Away Daily

Who does not like to receive a nice, warm, heart-felt hug? Very few people! Most of us, deep down love giving and receiving hugs from loved ones and friends.

Hugging is a great way of increasing mental or physical healing. Research shows that hugging is effective at healing or reducing depression, anxiety, stress and loneliness. It is also great at healing sickness and diseases.

Hugs are the next step up from a handshake. When you hold out your hand, everyone knows this is an invitation to shake hands. When it comes to hugs I always suggest that you ask permission first. This is especially important if it is not a close friend or family member.

Many people are not use to being hugged, so ask first, and then hug. You may have been raised in a family of non-huggers. If so, you may have to learn to hug and feel comfortable doing it. It just takes practice.

The type of hug I am talking about is a proper deep hug; one where the hearts are pressing together. Some people call this a 'Bear Hug'. Research is showing that this type of hug has the most benefits, such as:

1. First and foremost, the loving touch of a hug helps build a sense of safety and trust. A hug helps you to have an open and honest communication with others.

2. Hugs help increase your Oxytocin levels almost instantly. Oxytocin helps heal feelings of anger, loneliness and isolation.

3. Hugs help teach you that love flows both ways. Hugs also teach you how to give and receive. When embraced in a hug you are giving and receiving at the same time. There is equal value in giving and receiving.

4. Hugs are a lot like laughter and meditation. Hugs let you get out of your boring and routine thinking patterns so you can connect with your heart, your feelings and your breath. They allow you to feel joy and happiness in your heart. Hugs allow you to flow the energy of life between the two of you.

5. Serotonin (a feel good hormone) levels are increased when we hold a hug for more than a brief second. Your moods will elevate and help create more happiness. Let your hugs linger just a bit longer than a brief second.

6. Your self-esteem or self-worth gets a nice boost from hugging. Since you were a baby the touch from your family shows you that you are special and loved. There is a relationship between self-worth and physical sensations from your earliest years and that is still imbedded in your nervous system today. All those cuddles you received from your parents while growing up still remain imprinted at a cellular level. Hugs remind us at a physical level of those cuddling moments; therefore, hugs connect you to your ability to self-love.

7. Your muscles relax and tension is released from your body when you hug. Pain dissipates for a little while after a hug.

8. There is an energy that is exchanged between two people when they are hugging. This is an investment in that relationship. Hugs encourage understanding and empathy.

There is a synergistic effect, which means that 'the whole is greater than the sum of its parts'. This synergy can cause a win-win-win outcome – you, the other person and the relationship between the two of you all win.

9. Your immune (disease fighting) system is strengthened by hugs. The gentle pressure on your sternum and the emotional charge that is created helps stimulate your thymus gland (this regulates and balances your body's production of white blood cell, which keep you healthy and disease free).

Based on these 9 benefits, you can see that there are a lot of benefits from receiving and giving hugs.

Hugs improve relationships and elevate moods, so set a goal for how many hugs you will give a day. The bare minimum is 1 hug a day. Good: 4-5 hugs a day. Best: 6-12! To make this more of a challenge, give these hugs to different people and not just the same individuals each time. This will brighten your day and the other person's day.

Virginia Satir, is a highly respected family therapist and she had this to say about hugs.

"We need four hugs a day for survival. We need eight hugs a day for maintenance. We need twelve hugs a day for growth."

Action Item: Give away at least 2 hugs every day, and then work up from there. The goal is 8-12 a day. Remember to ask permission first.

SECRET #11 - TOUCH – Humans Thrive On Physical Touch

There is nothing more emotionally and physically healing than human touch. When we touch each other, there is a spiritual connection and an exchange of energy that is recognized at the subconscious level.

Humans need to feel physical touch. You have a deep need to be touched and also to touch others, even though you may know it. The other person also in return wants and need to be touched. We are talking appropriate touching, such as a hug (with permission), shaking hands, holding hands, lightly placing a hand on a shoulder or arm.

I have done a lot of work with the elderly through a service assignment in my church and I always shake their hands, hold their hands or lightly place my hand on their hands or arms when talking to them. I feel their love and they feel mine. We both benefit from this slight physical touch.

Research seems to back this all up!

At Duke University in North Carolina, research is showing that touch and massage can cut down on the levels of stress hormones. These elevated stress hormones are responsible for increasing your risk of a number of diseases and mood disorders. Touch seems to increase the levels of melatonin and serotonin.

The Touch Research Institute at the University Of Miami School Of Medicine says that they have performed more than 100 studies into human touch and found it has a major effect on the following:
- Faster growth in premature babies
- Reduced pain levels

- Lower glucose levels in children with diabetes
- Improves the immune system in people with cancer
- Decrease autoimmune disease symptoms.

As you can see, human touch has healing properties. You never know who might need a 'healing touch'. Touch spreads love, and love heals everything, so spread love wherever you go. Others will feel better and you will feel better.

ACTION ITEM: Start touching people in a natural, non-invasive way to let them know you care. Touch transmits love, and love heals everything.

SECRET #12 - LISTEN – Listen Twice As Much As You Talk

The title of this tip is a correct principle BUT when you are listening really listen. You have to not only hear what is being said, but more importantly you must <u>understand</u> what they are saying.

Listening skills is one of the most important talent you can develop. How well you listen has a major impact on your job effectiveness and on the quality of your relationships with parents, friends and others in your life.

There are 4 major reasons why we listen. We listen –
  o To obtain information
  o To Understand
  o For Enjoyment
  o To Learn

Improving your listening skills will help you at school, work and at home. Much of the stress in life comes from misunderstandings, either at school, at work with co-workers or at home with family members. Most of the misunderstandings come from not 'listening' to the other person. Yes, you may 'hear' them but did you listen to get all the information that they were trying to pass on to you?

Here are a couple of listening tips.

1. PAY ATTENTION - Give the speaker your undivided attention, and acknowledge the message.
2. SHOW THAT YOU ARE LISTENING - Use your body language and gestures to convey your attention, such as a slight nodding of the head.
3. PROVIDE FEED BACK - As a listener, your role is to understand what is being said. This may require you to reflect on what is being said and ask questions.
4. DO NOT INTERUPT or DEFER JUDGMENT - Interrupting is a waste of time. It frustrates the speaker and limits full understanding of the message.
5. APPROPRIATELY RESPOND - You are gaining information and the other person's viewpoint. You add nothing by attacking the speaker or otherwise putting him or her down.

If you will improve your listening skill and really listen to the one who is speaking, and listen twice as much as you talk, the relationships will improve. This improved relationship and improved effectiveness at school, work and home, will also help reduce stress. We know that stress leads to sickness, disease and depression.

So for your health and your happiness, LISTEN!!

ACTION ITEM: When someone is talking, implement these 5 tips. Listen and stop thinking about YOUR next response back. Remember – when the other person is talking, what they are saying is the most important thing going on at that moment.

SECRET #13 - FORGIVE OTHERS AND YOURSELF – Then Let It Go

Forgiveness – *The decision and act of letting go of and to stop feeling, angry, resentment and thoughts of revenge.*

The act of forgiveness can and will lessen the grip that someone, who has offended or hurt you, may have on you. You may not even know how much they have affected you until after you forgive them. Forgiveness will help you focus on other more positive parts of your life. When you forgive someone you do not necessarily forget the wrong that was done, but it can and will lead to feelings of empathy, compassion and understanding for the one who hurt you.

The Attitude of forgiving and forgiveness helps release stress that may be bottled up inside of you. Forgiveness is another great stress reliever.

This need to forgive is not just for the big things someone has done to you but also the little things, such as someone's mean comment or a rude act. You don't even have to forgive them in person. If someone cuts you off on the freeway, you just think to yourself (or you can say it out loud), 'you must have a good reason so I forgive you', **then let it go**.

There are two sides of the forgiveness coin. The other side of this forgiveness step is for YOU to apologize and ask for forgiveness, to all those that YOU may have offended. None of us is perfect and this includes you. Take responsibility for your words and actions and when you offend someone, or think you may have offended someone – apologize.

But here is the catch. You must feel truly sorry for whatever you have said or done. You must be sincere in your sorrow or regret and specifically, you need to ask for forgiveness and do it without making any excuses.

Remember one thing, the other person may or may not accept your apology and forgive you. You cannot force them to forgive you. It may take them time to be moved enough to forgive. What is important is that you sincerely apologize.

Now that you have apologized to the person that you may have treated badly, you must now forgive yourself! This is the hardest step for most people. You are your own worst critic. You should not judge yourself too harshly. You are human, and as such you will make mistakes.

Very often depression is the result of excessive self-criticism that takes place over an extended period of time. These self-criticisms are sometimes the result of guilty feelings, plus it is easy to go overboard on beating yourself up.

I can almost promise that as you let go of grudges and bad feelings towards another person and yourself, you will no longer let your life be defined by how you have been hurt. You stop being the victim. You might be lucky enough to find understanding and compassion.

So forgive others, apologize and forgive yourself, quickly.

ACTION ITEM: Forgive someone every day, including YOU. Apologize when necessary. Never carry guilt or anger in your heart for long.

SECRET #14 - EAT MEALS TOGETHER AS A FAMILY

Eating together as a family for most of you means with your parent(s), siblings or grandparents. You can even count eating school lunch with a few special friends if you have no family. But for most of you it would be with loved ones.

You are probably wondering why eating together as a family is so important. Well, most American families do not eat many meals together. Most families are lacking in face to face time and even do not have much meaningful conversations with each other. Dinner may be the only time during the day that you can sit down to eat and have a conversation with your family.

Dinner should be a time where family can come together to relax, laugh, recharge their physical and emotional batteries. You can catch up on the activities of all the family members. This is a great time to build a sense of who your family is and develop closeness to each other. Mealtime creates a feeling of togetherness and family unity.

I know that your family is probably extremely busy but if your family could eat 5 meals a week together, you and your family will receive some great benefits. Researchers have found the following benefits for eating at least 5 meals a week together.

- Builds a healthy body and brain
- Great for building family spirit
- Lower Teenage substance abuse and pregnancy
- Lower Depression rates in teenagers
- Increased self-esteem and grades in children and teens
- Diet is greatly improved – improved health condition
- Less Obesity and other eating disorders
- Conversation is better at building vocabulary than reading

There are also a few other benefits for parents and teenagers.

- Your moods are elevated and there is less depression and anxiety
- You will stay closer to each other than those teenagers who do not eat with their parents
- Eating together around the dinner table can be a great 'unifier', a place all family members can feel safe.

One last point – eating alone can feel very lonely and isolating. This can help foster depression, anxiety and other mood disorders. So if you are depressed, feeling down or upset with a family member, sitting down and eating with them or others helps heal the wounds of loneliness or anger.

"A Family That Eats Together Stays Together And All Members Are Healthier and Happier."

ACTION ITEM: Eat Dinner together as a family, around the table, today. Try for 5 or more home cooked Dinners (or other meals) a week as a family. Your body, mind, spirit and family will love you for it.

SECRET #15 - FRIENDSHIP – Quality Not Quantity

The research is in and it shows that if you have a strong social network of good, strong, positive and committed friends you have a significant increase in better health and living longer. The reverse is also true – if you are socially isolated, few to no friends, you have a higher risk of poor mental and physical health and a shorter lifespan.

Other scientific studies also show that a few good, close friends who have a positive outlook on life and are usually in a good mood can have a huge positive impact on you and the rest of the group. This is especially true if you or one of the others within your group is suffering from depression or illness. Having a small group of dedicated friends can help you heal faster from illness, surgery or a mood disorder.

Here is one more thing to think about concerning friends. Acquaintances are NOT Friends. Casual friends or acquaintances probably will not be there for you in times of physical or emotional hardships. Real friends will!

"To Get A Friend - You Have To Be A Friend"

Here is a story about how to be a friend – A story of a young man's SMILE during his hardship.

Jaden Hayes, a six year old boy, whose parents had both died, was understandably heartbroken. Even though his parents were gone, he was determined to go on living with joy and happiness. One day he told his aunt that he was 'sick and tired of seeing everyone so sad all the time.'

So he decided he wanted to help turn other people's frowns into smiles. So Jaden, at the age of 6, started a 'Smile Campaign'. So Jaden and his aunt started handing out toys. These toys were small rubber duckies, dinosaurs, etc. – in order to make people, who were not smiling, Smile. His goal was 33,000 people smiling. At the time of the story he had made about 500 people smile.

Jaden is proof that even if you are going through a tough time, you can still make a difference in someone else's life. This will help both you and the other person heal.

Smile often to others, even strangers, and you will feel better and so will the other person. Who knows, maybe that smile will be the start of another great friendship.

ACTION ITEMS: Using some of the previous tips do something today to strengthen the relationship with a close, dear friend. You might really need them someday. Smile and Say Hi to a stranger today and brighten both your days.

SECRET #16 - SURVIVING DIVORCE AND SEPERATION

You are NOT Alone

Did you know that the divorce rate for all marriages is 50% or so? This means that about 40% of all children are affected by divorce and separation. This equates to about 1.5 million children and teenagers who are affected. I know that there are times that you feel alone and that you feel like your life is all messed up.

You may be asking – How am I ever going to get through this and have a normal happy and healthy life. Let me give you a few healthy tips to survive the divorce and separation years:

1. *IT IS NOT YOUR FAULT:* There are many reasons parents go through a separation and divorce. Rarely is it directly related to children. Just know that it is not your fault and that you can't blame yourself or feel guilty.

2. *TALK OUT YOUR FEELINGS*: You need to find someone who understands what you are going though and talk things out with them. You need moral support and an opportunity to get your feelings out. It can be a friend, counselor or someone who has been down the divorce road before you.

3. *LOVE BOTH PARENTS:* Don't blame one or the other for the divorce. Know that it usually takes two to fight and dance. Love them both as much as you can. Do not let one or the other force you to choose between them. Pick both.

4. *DON'T BE A PAWN:* Try not to let either parent put you in the middle. Do not pass messages back and forth. Do not let them tear down the other in your present. Stand up and do not become the victim.

5. *BEING UPSET IS NORMAL:* At times you probably felt anger, sadness, anxiety, worry, lonely, scared and embarrassed. These feelings are normal. *There is one feeling that you should not feel and that is – guilty.* You will feel most all of these emotions as you go through all the changes during and after the divorce.

Dealing with all these different emotions will be one of the hardest things you will have to deal with. This is why you need to have a good support group to learn coping skills.

Know that all these tips in this book can and will help you make it through the tough times of going through these teen years.

ACTION ITEM: If you are a child whose parents have separated or divorced, find someone to talk to about your feeling and emotions. If your parents have not divorced, find a friend who needs your support and give then a listening ear.

SECRET #17 - THE INNER LOVE: Self-Love

"Before you can truly love someone else you must first love yourself."

Do you believe this is a true statement true? There are many different variations of this statement, but they are all true. The fact is you must love yourself before you can really love someone else.

Here is another quote that I recently read, *"Your relationship with others is a mirror or a reflection of your relationship with yourself."* In other words, if you have 'less than desirable' relationship with a loved one, please take a good hard look inside yourself. The problem could be the relationship you have with yourself. Take care of the relationship you have with yourself and the problems you may have with others just may disappear.

I know you like the good feelings you get when you do things for others. But doing things for others really does not bring you lasting happiness. What is more important is how you see yourself for doing the good deed for others. This really determines whether you are really feeling 'happy'.

There is a difference between the two. It is a good thing to help others but it is the reason or motivation behind it that really counts. Consider this for a moment.

Are you helping others just because you need to feel good about yourself? Do you need other people's feedback to feel good about yourself? If so, it is because you have a limited ability to feel good about yourself without this positive feedback! Or in other words – You Lack Self-Love!

What if you had more self-love and self-acceptance? If you did, all the positive feedback and responses that you may get when you help someone would not be so important to you.

Once you have found and develop love and acceptance for you, then the reason to help others changes from a form of self-gratification or self-love to doing it out of love for them and yourself.

Who you are, your true self, your inner goodness is found within your inner core or your divine nature. You do not have to be different to be worthy of your own love. Because of your divine nature you *are* love. You are a wonderful and beautiful light. Believe in yourself and let your love and light shine forth and do not try to bury that love and light.

Loving yourself is a journey, an ongoing process and even a lifetime pursuit – and it all starts with YOU. So give yourself a great big hug and a few words of encouragement and try some of the following tips.

- o Stop comparing yourself to others! You are a special and a unique individual. There is nobody like you. So only compare yourself with the only person looking back at you in the mirror. Be kind and gentle with that person.

- When you wake up every morning, look in the mirror and tell yourself something really positive. It can be an affirmation, positive feedback on how you handled a situation, just something positive and something that will make you smile.

- When you are having a fantastic day, sit down and write out a list of your best qualities and accomplishments. Then on those days that are less than amazing, pull out the list and read it.

Be patient but be persistent. Self-Love is a process and sometimes it can be a slow process, but keep taking steps forward. It takes daily practice and a life time to master but it can and must be mastered.

So be kind to yourself. Support yourself especially when facing hard times.

ACTION ITEM: Every morning give yourself a big hug and tell yourself something positive and that will make you smile. Remember – You have to love yourself before you can truly love someone else.

EDUCATION - CAREER

SECRET #18 - RELATIONSHIP WITH MONEY

Did you know that your relationship with money starts now as a teenager? Now is the time to develop a positive attitude about money and developing good money habits. IF you do nothing your attitude about money will be passed down to you from your parents. Do they have a good relationship with money?

This all starts on a subconscious belief level and is called Money Scripts. It is these subconscious money scripts that drive your financial behaviors and decisions.

Developing a poor relationship with money now can cause major stress in the future. As you may know, chronic stress can lead to mental and physical disorders and diseases. You must have a good, positive and strong relationship with money to reduce stress later in life.

Some signs of a good, healthy relationship with money may include the following:

- Having an attitude that money is not evil and be used for doing good things.
- Saving part of your money so you can meet your future goals and obtain some of your *wants*.
- Learning about debt and it proper use.
- Spending money based on your values, needs and on priorities.
- Having and sticking to a budget.
- Having a college fund for when you graduate from high school.

If you spend money on impulse, have no budget or emergency funds and have a bad attitude about money, then you really need to work on your relationship with money.

Here are a couple of ideas to get you started.

- Attitude – It is all about Attitude. First be very thankful for everything you <u>do have</u> and worry less about what you <u>don't have</u>.

- WANTS and NEEDS – There is a difference. NEEDS are things like basic food, shelter, clothing, transportation and a job. WANTS are things like the latest smart phone, gaming devise, and wearing all the latest top name brand clothes. You must know and understand the difference between NEEDS and WANTS.

Life will go a little smoother, with less stress and with more happiness, when you have a great relationship with money.

Action Item: List your needs and wants. Then prioritize the wants. Try setting aside a little money each month towards the purchase of the #1 item on your 'Wants' List.

SECRET #19 - 7 GOAL SETTING TIPS FOR TEENAGERS

As teenagers it is possible to accomplish anything you want, as long as you set your mind to it and have a plan.

Research has shown that most all individuals who succeed in life have a plan and a support system. You probably already have a support team – family and close friends. Now you just need a plan to achieve your goals. Here are 7 steps to take to successfully accomplish your goals:

1. IDENTIFY – FOCUS: Identify and write down, in detail, your long-term goal or desire. Then stay focused on this goal. Don't forget to write down the purpose or reason for the goal.

2. BREAK IT DOWN TO STEPS: Break down the large goal into small, achievable steps. These steps can be weekly and monthly steps for the next 3 – 6 months. Be specific!

3. ACCOUNTABILITY: Find someone that can and will hold you accountable. Then report or check in with them on a daily or weekly basis.

4. MOTIVATION – INSPIRATION: Find supporters who will support you and cheer you on. Tell these supporters what is motivating you to take on this goal so they can remind you often.

5. HOPE: Reward yourself with mini-rewards when you complete each step along the way. Each time you accomplish one of the small steps toward your goal it will give you hope that the goal will become a reality.

6. COMMITMENT: You show your commitment level when you get back up and try again when you fail to meet one of the short term goals or steps. Then you take some time to re-evaluate:

a. Was the goal achievable given the situation?
b. If it was not, break that goal down into even smaller steps.
c. If the goal was achievable then you need to give up something for not meeting the goal.

7. SUCCESS: Keep track of all the small steps or short term goals. When you achieve or complete each small step take a moment and acknowledge it and maybe give yourself a small reward. Let your support members know about the small successes so they can join your mini-celebration.

If you follow these 7 simple steps you can accomplish anything. Give it a try.

ACTION ITEM: Set an achievable goal this week using the 7 simple goal setting and achieving steps. Go out and accomplish something this week that you have been putting off. You can do it!

SECRET #20 - JOB HUNTING FOR TEENS

"YOUR JOB DOES NOT DEFINE YOU, BUT HOW YOU DO IT DOES."

It is during your teenage years that you should start to pay for some of your own expenses, saving for college and learning about money. To do this you have to have a job. Most teens start off with summer jobs.

Most people have to either work for someone else or own a business for 30-40 years and then retire. It will probably be the same for you. Since you will be spending a lot of time on the job it will be best if you can find happiness and fulfilment from your job.

It is during your teenage years that you can try different jobs to see which industry or career you would like to pursue when you get out of high school. It can help you decide which college degree that you want to go after.

Here are some job-hunting tips:

- First look into the industry that you have an interest or hobby in. If you love to work in the yard or garden then think about looking for a job at the local nursery.
- Find opportunities to volunteer in your community. This will give you some experience plus something to put on your resume.
- Learn how to network. This is the old fashioned way – asking everyone you know if they have openings where they work or if they know of a job opening somewhere.
- Be thinking about how you can prepare yourself so you can improve your odds of getting the job you want. List all of your strong points and how you can be an asset to an employer. These are good points to put on a resume.
- Practice going through the job interview. Try to get as many interviews as possible. If you don't get the job after the first couple of interviews, learn from them and figure out how to improve for the next interview.

If you are just starting your teenage years, consider starting out babysitting some of the neighborhood kids or mowing some of the neighbors' yards. There are a lot of different ways to earn money in the early teen years. Talk to your parents or grandparents for ideas.

ACTION ITEM: If you currently do not have a job, use one of the tips above to start laying the ground work to obtain a job or earning an income.

SECRET #21 - START PLANNING AHEAD FOR THE FUTURE! It is never too early.

Now that you are a teenager I am sure you have been asked the old familiar questions – "What do you want to be when you grow up" or "What do you want to study when you go to college" and lets not leave out, "What do you plan on doing with your life?"

Thinking ahead is not a bad idea but don't let people put too much pressure on you too early. Sometimes it takes time to figure out the answers to these questions. It would be good to start doing some planning or at least figure out some different options.

Here are three helpful ways to get started:

Know Your Strengths – Work On Your Weaknesses

To answer the question- 'what do you want to do with your life,' you have to know your strengths and weaknesses. The strengths would include such things as, what you are good at and what you are passionate about. Weaknesses are just opportunities for growth and learning.

One way to help figure all this out is to list all your strengths and passions. If you can't think of any start asking your parents, siblings and friends what they think your strengths are and put them on the list. Then look at the list and try to think about which jobs or careers best match up with your abilities and strengths.

Here is one example: If you are naturally a compassionate person and are good at biology AND you love animals then you might consider becoming a veterinarian.

IF you are having a hard time with this part and you are starting to feel down about the future talk to your career or guidance counselor at school. They should have different aptitude tests that you can take to give you some ideas about your possible strengths.

Know What Your Options Are

You might think it is better to 'just get through high school graduation first.' It really is better to be thinking about your future and if you want to pursue a college education or jumping right into your career.

You really need to be thinking ahead especially if you are thinking about going to college. You need to think about what to possibly major in. IF you can decide early you can start to take some of the basic college courses while you are still in high school.

There are a lot of questions that need answers so start thinking about college and which college you might want to attend and then how you are going to pay for it. There are a lot of financial options available.

An alternative to college is vocational or technical colleges where you can go and learn a trade. You can learn to be a plumber, electrician, welder, carpenter or hair stylist. So for those of you who do not want to go to college this is a great option. It is also less expensive than college.

Other options may include joining the military. You can serve your country while learning valuable skills that can be used after military service. Or you can take a year off after high school graduation to get a job and save money and take a little time to figure things out.

Ask For Help And Guidance

Don't be afraid to ask a lot of questions and seek out help and guidance from adults. Here are a couple of ideas that might help:

Interview People – Interview someone in the field that you are considering. Like the example above, if you are thinking about becoming a veterinarian interview a couple of them. Ask what they love about their profession and what they don't like about it.

Shadow People – See if you can spend the day observing a person within the career you are looking at. See if you can spend a day shadowing a veterinarian, hair stylist, plumber, etc. This will give you a real feel what the job will be like. You might be surprise how many people will let you do that. At least ask!

The future is like putting together a puzzle. There can be a few pieces or a lot of pieces but you can put the puzzle pieces together by studying the picture and when needed asking for a little help.

Remember, you are the creator of your destiny, not your friends, parents or the school guidance counselor. Do not be afraid to create your own destiny!

ACTION ITEM: This week think about your strengths and passions. Then write them down on paper. Then take a look at the list and write down all the different jobs or careers that match up with your strengths.

SECRET #22 - ENTREPRENEURSHIP – Is It For You

Have you ever dreamed of owning your own business, or thought it would be great to be your own boss? Many business owners absolutely love what they are doing. They will tell you that it is not a piece of cake? They will all tell you that it can be stressful, a lot of work, and even discouraging at times. But they will quickly tell you that it is worth it.

If you think you would like to own your own business and become an entrepreneur why not start now as a teenager! Starting a business does not have to be complicated but it does take a little money, time and a whole lot of commitment and perseverance. But you can do it.

There are plenty of examples of teens starting business and being highly successful, even millionaires by their early 20's. Having an online business makes it much easier for teenagers to start a business. You can create tee shirts and sell online or start a blog or even podcasting. The ideas are endless with an online business.

Another advantage of having your own business is there are some long term health benefits such as:

- Many business owners are healthier than the average wage earner.
- On average, business owners eat healthier than non-business owners.
- Entrepreneurs exercise more, up to 30 minutes 3-5 times a week.
- Entrepreneurs are more optimistic about the future.
- Once the business is established they have more free time to enjoy life.

The results? Entrepreneurs were the healthiest group in essentially every area. These individuals had much lower rates of mental illnesses such as depression and anxiety (the two leading mental health issues in the world today), less physical illnesses such as high blood pressure, hypertension, lower rates of hospital visits and they just felt better all the way around.

As you can see, entrepreneurship has some very positive, healthy as well as income advantages. But again you have to be doing something that you love doing and providing a product or service that you are passionate about. It will be worth your time to research what it will take to start a business. You never know, you might become a very successful teenager - business owner.

ACTION ITEM: Read a book about how to start and run your own business. See if you have the passion, determination and personality to be an entrepreneur. OR   List subjects that you are passionate about and have expertise in. Then research business ideas that are within that subject area.

SECRET #23 - FIND THE WORK YOU LOVE THROUGH VOLUNTEERING

2,500 years ago Aristotle gave us one of the best career advices ever given –

"Where the needs of the world and your talents cross, there lies your vocation."

This is true even for teens who are trying to figure out their career paths. Look to being a volunteer to help find the answers.

Did you know that today's teenagers are more civic minded than earlier generations of teens? It seems that this generation wants to make a difference in the world and they are looking to volunteering to fill that need. Giving back to your community and helping others is a great way to make a difference.

Volunteering is a great way to get experience to help get a job or to get into college. When you get involved in helping to promote a good cause you can be trying out career options.

Think about this – if you are thinking about becoming a veterinarian you can volunteer to work at an animal shelter. If you love sports then volunteer at a local YMCA. If you love the outdoors then look at the Sierra Club. Are you good with word and building tools, try helping with **Habitat for Humanities**. I think you get the point. Use your community serve to see if that is an area you would like to make your career.

There are many other BENEFITS to volunteering such as:

- Gain some leadership skills and boost your confidence.
- Skill and talent development for future job or career.
- Improving education while boosting your resume.
- Add to the list of recommendations for college application or future employment.
- Increasing your circle of influence by meeting new people.
- Make a difference in the lives of other and in a small way have a positive impact in the world.

Harvard University professor Howard Gardner said,

'The best alternative is to find an ethical career, focused on values and issues that matter to YOU, and which also allows you to do what you're really good at.'

Volunteering is a great way to find an ethical career, making a difference and doing what you love and you are good at. This is a great recipe for finding a job you love.

When you work at a job or in a career that you love you will be healthier and happier.

ACTION ITEM: This week search out different volunteering opportunities in your community. Find one you would like to try and contact them.

SECRET #24 - PASSIONS AND HOBBIES

For many people, including teens and this may include you, would love to turn a passion or a hobby into a business or a source of income. This would be an ideal situation for finding a job or career that you could love.

Do you know the difference between a hobby and a passion?

Let's take a minute and find out.

HOBBY – is a pursuit or activity that is outside of school or work that is engaged in for relaxation. If you are doing something you enjoy, but not many people are willing to pay for doing it, this is a hobby and not a sustainable career.

With a hobby there are two different approaches – you either need to work hard, learn more skills, knowledge or experience until people will pay you for it. OR be content to keep it as a hobby purely for your enjoyment and relaxation.

PASSION – they don't leave you alone and are generally not relaxing. A Passion pushes itself in your life even if you don't have time for them. Passions will soothe you and at the same time can drive you crazy.

Passions are so much more than just a mere interest. To have a passion for something is to have a very strong interest. For some people, the passion almost takes over their lives. If you are passionate about something, you spend all or most of your free time on it. You are learning all you can and enhancing your skills in this area. You are always thinking about what you are going to do next with it. With a passion, you are not afraid to work for it, and in fact you never consider IT work, but a pleasure to do.

So, what are you willing to sacrifice time, money, sleep or a vacation for? What is the activity or area that you just can't stay away from? The answer would be your passion!

NOTE: There is a difference between Passion and Compulsion! You can control a passion, you can't control a compulsion. Know the difference. Compulsions control your life and are very negative. Passions and hobbies should be relaxing, refreshing, and pleasurable and can be turned into businesses and careers.

The whole idea behind this secret is that it is possible to develop a hobby and turn it into a passion. This new passion can then be turned into a career. Those who can do this will find more peace, fulfillment and happiness in their career. It is critical to your overall health and happiness to have a job or career that you love. Even if you feel that you cannot turn your hobby or passion into an income, you still must have a hobby to make life a little more relaxing and enjoyable.

ACTION ITEM: Take a look at all your different activities and see which ones are hobbies and which ones are passions. Then evaluate to see if you can turn either into a source of income.

SECRET #25 - EDUCATION – The Road Away From Poverty

"Education is better than playing the lottery if you want to have a nice lifestyle throughout adulthood."

Stay in school! Graduate from high school! Adults without a high school diploma rarely get much above poverty level income. High school diploma is good – Trade School is better – A College degree is best if you can.

Just in case you did not know - the more education you can get the better job you can qualify for. Research and statistics back up this idea.

- If you only have a high school education, you are ½ as likely to make over $40,000 a year compared to those with a college degree.

- If you have a college degree, you are nearly 9 times more likely to make over $100,000 a year and 13 times more likely to earn over $200,000 compared to someone with just a high school diploma

- By 2020 it is forecast that nearly 2/3 of all occupations in the U.S. will require a college degree.

A less expensive option is a two-year degree or trade certifications and many of these pay $50,000-$60,000 a years after a couple of years' experience. Check out your local community college and see what they have to offer.

Make sure you graduate from high school with the best grades you can get. Then set the target for additional education at a Vocational School or College.

NEVER STOP LEARNING! LEARNING IS A LIFETIME PERSUIT!

EDUCATION IS THE PATH TO A FINANCIALLY STABLE LIFE.

ACTION ITEM: Set a written goal to graduate from high school. If you are in high school take a pre-college or college course to get a jump ahead.

PHYSICAL ACTIVITY (EXERCISE)

SECRET #26 - 30 MINUTES A DAY

The #1 health issue facing teenager now is overweight and obesity. The two main reasons for this are poor diet and lack of exercise or physical activity. Texting, playing electronic games is NOT exercising.

Both webmd.com and the Mayo Clinic support the exercise recommendations of the U.S. Dept. of Health and Human Services. These are recommendations that will help maintain a good healthy body and mind. Their recommendations are minimums – more will be required for weight-loss:

- o Moderate Aerobic Activities – 30 minutes a day or 150 minutes a week. This type of activity would include – brisk walking, swimming, and mowing the lawn (riding lawn mowers do not count).
- o Vigorous Aerobic Exercise – 15 minutes a day or 75 minutes a week. This type of activity would include running or aerobic dancing.
- o Strength Training – Twice a week. There is no specific amount of time for each session. This type of activity would include weight machines or weight bearing exercises.

Here are three tips to help you implement 30 minutes of physical activities into your day:

1. Physical activities do not mean you have to "exercise". Make a list of physical activities you enjoy doing. Start doing some of these every day.
2. Involve others. Do these activities as a family or with a group of friends. This way all of you will benefit from the activity.

3. Start simple - take the stairs, park farther away and walk, or take short walks around your school building during lunch.

Starting small and working up is simple to do and the health benefits are tremendous. Everyone knows exercise is good for them but few seem to put forth the effort. Your reward for adding more physical activities into your day life is great health and happiness. It is very hard to be happy when you feel tired and out of energy. Your body, mind and moods will love you for your efforts.

ACTION ITEM: Add more movement and physical activities into your daily routine. Strive for 30 total minutes a day of physical activities such as walking, taking the stairs or simple exercises.

SECRET #27 - EXERCISE: VARIETY = SUSTAINABILITY

Variety is the spice of life when it comes to sticking to an exercise plan.

Scientific studies support this idea. Many teens start an exercise routine but quit after a few days or weeks. Now the prevailing wisdom is to add variation to your exercise routine to help keep exercising. This is according to a University of Florida study.

This study was published in the Journal of Sport Behavior. The researchers took 114 men and women and put them into three categories or groups: Group 1 – exercise was varied. Group 2 – performed the same set of exercises and Group 3 – no set schedule or regulations.

Results: At the end of the study, there were only 61 of the 114 original members. 52 members had dropped out and one was disqualified. This left 24 people in the first group, 22 in the second group and only 15 in the third group. According to the researcher the highest dropout rate was with the 3rd group – with no schedule or regulations.

After the study researchers had the following tips and ideas;

- Do whatever it take to keep your routine from getting boring and monotonous
- Doing cardio (aerobic) exercises one day then the next day doing strength training (lifting weights or similar activity) and next day working on flexibility (stretches, yoga, qi gong) and alternating these three is the best routine for overall health, wellness and weight loss
- It can be as simple as going for a walk one day, running the next and then aerobics. Just mix it up
- Try new things. Try swimming, hiking, basketball... you get the idea
- Involve someone else – family member or a friend

Again, research proves that you will stick with exercising IF you make it fun, mix it up and involve others. In the end, it will be your willingness to try new things that will keep boredom away and increase your dedication to exercising... which will pay great dividends, including weight-loss, happier moods and overall better health.

ACTION ITEM: Mix it up by trying more new exercises, while keeping with those you found to be enjoyable. Your willingness to try new exercises or physical activities will lead to compliance and sustainability.

SECRET #28 - QIGONG – Movements For Health

The word Qigong (Chi Kung, Qigung) has two parts – Qi and Gong.

Qi is pronounced as 'Chee" which is translated to mean – *Life Force or Vital-Energy*. The Chinese believe this Life Force or Vital-Energy flows through all things in the universe.

Gong is pronounced as 'gung' and is translated to mean – **Skill or Accomplishment that is cultivated through steady practice**.

Qigong = Cultivating Life Force Energy

What is Qigong?

It is part of an ancient Chinese health system. It has been practiced by the Chinese for centuries and goes back for several thousand years. Every day it is practiced by 10's of millions of people all around the world.

There are hundreds of variations of Qigong but most all the types have the same three components:

- o Postures – Movements
- o Breathing techniques
- o Mental Focus or Visualization

Most of the Qigong forms are slow and gentle movements that are easily adaptable and can even be done by the physically challenged and can be practiced by the old as well as the young. In China all ages, from the little children to the oldest sages, practice Qigong.

It is a system that is practiced to increase vitality and to promote healing and maintaining good health.

Qigong helps promote mental clarity, good health and has been shown to be effective in relieving a variety of ailments, including stress. Scientific research has shown that stress is a major contributing factor in depression, high blood pressure, asthma and heart disease, to list just a few issues. Because there is a lot of interest around the world in relieving stress, people are looking into the healing properties of Qigong. It is sometimes called **'moving meditation.'**

You will have a more positive outlook on life, and harmful attitudes, moods and behaviors will be eliminated, when the three characteristics of Qigong are put into the session. Incorporating Qigong into your daily routine will help create a well-balanced life. When your life is more in balance it will bring greater harmony, stability and enjoyment into your daily life.

As you add the practice of Qigong into your daily life you will improve your physical health, mental health and your emotional health. In other words, you will improve your health and happiness in your life.

ACTION ITEM: Learn the Shibashi 18 Movements. Easy to learn and powerful, you will see great results.

SECRET #29 - YOGA – You Are Limber Enough

Yoga is part of the ancient healing art in India just as Qi Gong is in China. Both countries and cultures use different movements and poses to heal the mind and body.

Yoga is very popular and is practiced by athletes, children, seniors and people of all walks of life. Yoga can be modified to suit all levels of fitness, from beginners to the expert. It has been proven to lower blood pressure, increase flexibility and strength, and to reduce stress levels. Yoga calms the mind and energizes the body and mind.

So what exactly is Yoga? The word Yoga is derived from the Sankrit word "yuj" which means "to unite or integrate"; yoga is 5000 years old.

Most people picture an individual in weird, twisted and seemingly impossible poses. It is that and a lot more. Because of the poses many people feel they cannot do Yoga. I for one am older and not very flexible and it is nearly impossible for me to do most of the poses. For this reason I stick with Qi Gong. But again Yoga is much more than the poses.

But as a teenager you are much more flexible and should be able to do all the beginner poses and movements and then work up to more advanced levels if you find Yoga enjoyable.

Yoga, for many people is a way of life, but for the rest of us it is way to relax, stretch and harmonize the body with the mind. Yoga does this through three main processes:

- Various Breathing Techniques (discussed in a later secret)
- Yoga Postures (your body needs to be pretty flexible to do many of these poses)

- Meditation (discussed in another secret)

When your body, mind and spirit are in harmony within you, your journey through life becomes a little calmer, happier and more fulfilled. There are many, many studies that show that Yoga helps heal so many different physical, mental and emotional issues that everyone can benefit from adding Yoga into their daily routine.

Here are some physical benefits of Yoga:

- Increased flexibility
- Improved muscle tone and strength
- Respiration, Vitality and Energy levels are improved
- A balanced metabolism and weight reduction
- Improved Circulatory and Cardio health

Beside these and many other physical benefits, one of the best or well-known benefits has to do with stress management. Stress as you may be well aware of, has a major impact on the body and mind. Stress is a major contributor to depression, anxiety, sleep disorders, and lack of concentration, just to list a few.

So to sum things up – "Yoga is effective in developing coping skills and reaching a more positive outlook on life."

Remember: Your body is your best guide. You don't have to stick to one kind of yoga, just do what your body needs, and try different types until you find one you like! Yoga can be one important step toward finding health and happiness. Try it! You just might like it!

ACTION ITEM: Find a local Yoga studio and register for a class or order a training video and try Yoga in the privacy of your own home. Your body is flexible enough to do this.

SECRET #30 - THE BRAIN – It Needs Exercise Too

"If Your Brain Is Not Healthy And Happy – NOBODY Is Happy!"

Your brain is just like a muscle in your body. If you work it – it will grow and get stronger. If you do not use it – it will shrink and grow weaker. As a teenager your brain is still growing and maturing. Many scientific studies show that the brain is not fully grown or mature until about age 21. The growth of new brain cells and neurotransmitters is called neuroplasticity.

After the age of 21 or when there is repeated head trauma, brain cells are damaged and die. This damage does not normally show any visible signs of slowing down or memory loss at first. This happens slowly through the years, until it is almost too late. This lack of concentration or memory loss makes it hard to perform mental tasks.

As your brain cells and neurotransmitters are created and strengthened, you start to build up your 'cognitive reserves' or the brains ability to withstand damage due to aging, stress and other factors.

Researchers now believe that if you will implement a brain-healthy lifestyle and exercise you can increase your brain's cognitive reserves. This is just like adding weight training for your muscles and building them up to help you retain more muscles as you get older.

Here is a short list from a very long list of idea to give your brain a workout that goes beyond a healthy diet and normal physical exercise:

- Learn Music – Join a choir or learn to play a musical instrument.
- Learn A Language – This can be sign language or a foreign language. Make sure it is something you can use with people who live around you. It will make learning easier and fun.
- Start a new hobby that involves fine-motor skills which help refine your hand-eye capabilities. This could include drawing, painting, assembling a puzzle or knitting. You get the idea.
- Use your other hand. Brush your teeth or any other task with the 'other hand' or non-dominant hand.
- Break out of your Routine. Switch up your morning activities or other parts of your daily routine. Drive to or from school or work a different way.

Your brain is like your body – it does not function well in a boring, non-stimulating routine. So for your brains sake – mix it up a bit.

Bonus Tip!

Rewire your brain for More Happiness – Take In and Enjoy the Good in Life

I know that you encounter a few positive moments throughout each day. Many of these moments are small or seem to be insignificant, but they can be critical in changing your viewpoint on life and how the brain works. To do this you must take the time to:

- Appreciate the positive moments – moments of joy, happiness
- Increase the Intensity and Duration of these moments in your mind

We do this by lingering on them longer. Enjoy the moment and really feel the joy and happiness of experience. This is very effective in helping the brain to 'rewire' itself from a natural bias toward negativity to a more positive bias.

Researchers tell us now that when you appreciate and maximize the small, positive experiences, "...increasingly there's a sense of being filled up already inside, or already feeling safe inside, or already feeling loved and liked and respected. So we have less of a sense of striving...' Insecurity falls away because you've got the good stuff inside of yourself.

> "The more that things seem fresh and new, the more that you're looking at them with a beginner's mind or child's mind, that's going to increase brain structure because the brain is always looking for what's new."

So, break the routine and do things a little different every day AND linger longer on the positive experiences that you have throughout your day and you will have a strong, healthy and happy brain.

ACTION ITEM: Change up your daily routine – brush your teeth with the 'other' hand. Find ways to mix things up a little and stay away from doing everything the same way each time..

Take an extra minute or to think about and appreciate, all the little positive experiences, thoughts or moments. This will help the brain grow more 'positive' neurons.

SECRET #31 - DAILY WALKS – BungyPump Walking

Going on daily walks has been promoted by health care professionals for years. You may have taken an occasional walk through your neighborhood. There are indeed health benefits from leisure walks. But if you want to spice up those walks a little bit you have to try BungyPump walking.

These special walking poles were developed a few years ago and are manufactured in Sweden. These poles have quickly spread across Europe and they are sold in the U.S.

BungyPump fitness poles help transform a normal walk or easy hike into a complete body workout that will exercise 90% of your muscles. Compared to going on a normal walk, these fitness poles will burn up to 77% more calories. You know that burning calories leads to weight loss.

They have rigid or solid walking sticks used in Nordic Walking or hiking. The BungyPump poles have a featured 'built-in suspension system', that provides smooth and steady resistance every time the poles are pressed down, without any straining or jarring movements.

The pole height is adjustable. The poles come with different amounts of resistance. They vary from 8, 13, and 22 pounds.

The 8 pound resistance is for beginners. The 22 pounder is for seasoned athletes or very active individuals.

Watch these informative videos to see the BungyPump™ in action. (http://thehealthybabyboomer.com/bungypump/)

Mile for mile, using the BungyPump is 30% more efficient than walking without them. It is fun and enjoyable. I love mine. Put the 'spring' back into your walks and watch your body tone up and moods soar.

ACTION ITEM: Check the link above and find out more about the BungyPumps and see them in action. Then go out for a walk.

SECRET #32 - STRENGTH TRAINING

When it comes to your muscles - USE IT OR LOSE IT!

Strength Training: A type of physical exercise specializing in the use of resistance to induce muscular contraction which builds strength, anaerobic endurance, and size of skeletal muscles.

Not all types of exercises are designed to build and strengthen muscles. Aerobics are designed to burn calories, build your heart muscles and increase blood flow throughout the body. You need to build up your muscles to keep them toned for work and play.

Here is a short list of benefits of strength training:

- Helps control your weight. Muscles are more efficient at burning calories than any other part of your body. So the more toned your muscles, the easier it is to control your weight.
- Helps improve depression as well as anti-depressant medications. When you participate in strength training programs, your self-confidence and self-esteem improve, which helps increase your overall quality of life and happiness.

- Helps develop strong bones. By stressing your bones, strength training increases bone density and reduces the risk of bones breaking.
- Helps boost your stamina. As you get stronger, you won't fatigue as easily. Building muscle also contributes to better balance.

Strength Training can be done at a gym or you can easily do them in the privacy of your own home. There are 4 common types of strength training:

1. Body Weight - Basically you are using your body as the weights or resistance. These would be exercises like squats, crunches, planks, pushups, etc. There are hundreds of variations of these types of strength training exercises.
2. Resistance Tubing – Resistance tubing is inexpensive, light weight and come in many different types and resistance levels. Found in most sporting goods stores.
3. Free Weights or Weight Lifting – This is the most commonly thought of strength training. This type uses barbells and dumbbells.
4. Weight Machines – Most gyms and fitness centers offer different resistance or weight lifting machines. You can even buy them for home use.

So add some strength or resistance training into your exercise schedule for a happier and healthier life.

ACTION ITEM: Experiment with some of the different types of strength or resistance training to see which one you like. Then start doing strength training 2-3 times a week.

SECRET #33 - THE ELECTRONIC DETOX

Digital detox: *A period of time during which a person refrains from using electronic devices such as smartphones or computers, regarded as an opportunity to reduce stress or focus on social interaction in the physical world.*

- Oxford English Dictionary, 2013

The Relationship that teenagers and adults have with technology is not always the healthiest. There are the seemingly endless hours of texting, scanning Facebook and other social media outlets, checking emails not to mention hours of sitting in front of the TV.

This digital baggage that you may carry with you every hour of every day can have a negative effect on your health and wellbeing such as:

- Headaches caused by eye strain
- Usage before bed causes poor sleep by disrupting the production of melatonin
- Addiction – 44% of cell phone owner sleep with their cellphones next to their bed so they don't miss anything.
- Lower self-esteem because of people comparing themselves with others on Facebook
- Poor relationships with others because of 'lack of face to face time' and communication.

There are a lot of scientific studies that support the above point plus dozens of other negative outcomes. If you really take a good hard, realistic look at yourself I think you will find that you can contribute some of the negativity with your health and other area of your life to excess time with electronic devices.

The mere fact that you can now find the phrase 'digital detox' in the Oxford Dictionary is proof enough that many people have a need to take a break.

Here are a few steps to accomplishing an Electronic Detox:

1. Get Excited – This will be a great learning experience. One for the journal. So get excited about the possibilities.
2. Pick A Time Period - The first real step is to pick a time frame for the detox. It needs to a challenge but also realistic. **Hint:** Try for a full weekend – Friday Night to Monday Morning. It really needs to be long enough to unwind and disconnect.
3. Set Boundaries – The first electronic detox might include anything with a glowing screen or the internet, such as the TV, computer, smart phones, iPad, etc.
4. Schedule Time With Loved Ones And Friends – During the detox schedule time to get together with family and friends. Schedule a meal together WITHOUT cellphones, etc.. HINT: Try pulling out an old board game and have some real fun and laughs.
5. Get Outdoors - Here is a chance to get outdoors. In fact make this a mandatory requirement each time you do this. This can be a hike, a walk on the beach, a picnic at the park or any other fun outdoor activity that you enjoy. An added benefit is you will get a nice dose of Vitamin D!
6. Read A Real Book Or Magazine - Use this detox time to enjoy a nice real book or real magazine, ones that you hold in your hands and turn pages. Some people believe that people are losing their "capacity for concentration and contemplation" because of spending too much time on the internet.
7. What Did You Learn – When the detox time is up take a few minutes to think about your experience before rushing to

your electronic devices. Write down and answer the following 3 questions:

1. What have I learned from this experience?

2. Now that I have lived without my electronic devices for this long, is there any device/platform or social media I can do without permanently?

3. Would I consider doing this on a regular schedule (say, Saturday afternoon to Sunday evening every week) to repeat the experience?

There are many benefits to doing an electronic detox, especially if it is on a regular basis (a weekend a month). Try it!

ACTION ITEM: Using the tips above, pick a weekend and do your first electronic detox and see how you feel.

SPIRITUALITY:

SECRET #34 - WHAT DOES SPIRITUALITY MEAN TO YOU?   DEFINE IT!

"Those who have a strong spiritual foundation tend to heal quicker and are generally healthier, both in mind and body, compared to those who do not have spirituality in their lives."

This statement comes from personal experience and training, many scientific studies, and the experience of thousands of health practitioners and health coaches. The research is there to support this opening statement, if one will put forth the time to look for it. But first you need to define what spirituality means to you.

'Spirituality can be a broad concept that has room for different viewpoints. Generally speaking, it includes a sense of connection or close association with something much bigger than you, and it generally involves a search for some meaning in life. It is something that touches all of us and as such is a universal human experience.'

Spirituality has different meanings to different people. But before you can improve or strengthen your spirituality you must be able to define it – for you. I know what it means to me, and for me it includes being active in my religious community or church and a strong belief in God or a Heavenly Father.

Here is a couple of different concepts or ideas of spirituality.

1. Non-religious or secular individuals see spirituality as nothing more than, 'an inner path enabling a person to discover the

core of his/her being...aspects of life and human experience which go beyond a purely materialistic view of the world without necessarily accepting belief in a supernatural reality or divine being. Some look to the power of vibrations of the universe as the supreme power.'

2. Christians and other religions reject the previous idea of spirituality. I fall into this group. Spirituality among Christians and others vary widely, but have one thing in common – it involves our relationship, to some level, with a personal creator, God or Heavenly Father who exists outside of us and has revealed himself to us at some level.

3. Spirituality - includes the body, mind, soul and relationships or in other words, the whole person. It also includes all aspects of your life, and is a lived experience. Think of it as a journey throughout your life that involves the elements of values and beliefs. These elements help motivate you to grow, develop and expand your life; causing a transformation of your consciousness and thus your life. This can involve the knowing and experiencing God, not just knowing about God or the higher power of the Universe.

Talk to your parents, friends and other what their thoughts are about spirituality. This could give you a starting place if you are growing up in a family without a religious foundation.

You might find yourself in one of these areas or a combination. You must have a set of core values and know where they originated. Either way, your health and happiness can really be affected by your level of spirituality. Your body, mind and spirit will love you if you will strengthen your spirituality.

SECRET #35 - WHAT IS MY LIFE PURPOSE?

Even though you are just starting out in life, you must develop a strong sense of who you are and what your purpose is here on this earth. Depression, anxiety, or having poor health can suck the life out of you; leaving you feeling like your life is pointless. In general, life can seem empty and meaningless at times, because we just let life happen. Questions about the meaning of life are a profound issue that is facing all of humanity.

There is no one right answer or predetermined meaning to life that applies to you and everyone else. It is up to you to find the answers and it is also up to you to make your life meaningful and have a purpose. Nobody can do it for you! When it comes to societies and communities, everyone will have to find how best to work together to build meaningful futures.

It is very important that you have a strong core belief system and to really understand this belief system and how it relates to your purpose of life. If you do know and understand, then when those dark days come into your life, you will know who you are and what your purpose or mission is.

Emily Deans, M.D., a well-seasoned and experienced clinician had this to say,

"Religion and Spirituality are an important part of many people's lives, and in my experience, it can lend to significant benefits in resiliency (resistant to future episodes). I've seen non-spiritual folk struggle more, perhaps, with feelings they are unloved and unworthy when traumatized than those with a spiritual "back-up" who feel that, no matter what happens, they have a spiritual connection to something greater. In addition, the spiritual and religious don't seem to wrestle as much with those existential questions of 'why am I here? What is my purpose?' that can plague the non-spiritual."

For your own peace of mind, you need to decide, <u>for yourself</u>, what you are supposed to accomplish while you are alive on this planet. When you can answer this question, you will be more at peace within yourself and with all those people around you, and your life will have much more meaning and purpose.

ACTION ITEM: On deep spiritual topics you need to take time to do some deep soul searching. Take some time to ponder this question – What is my purpose in life? What is my mission (what am I to accomplish) in this life?

SECRET #36 - WHERE DID I COME FROM? – IS THERE LIFE AFTER DEATH?

These questions have been pondered, debated and the answers even fought over since the beginning of time. But if you can study, ponder and come to an understanding of what the answers to these questions mean to you, life will have greater meaning.

Wikipedia had this to say – "Pre-existence, Beforelife, Pre-mortal Existence refers to the belief that each individual human soul or spirit existed before mortal conception, and at some point before birth, this spirit or soul enters or is placed into the body. Concepts of pre-existence can encompass either the belief that the soul came into existence at some time prior to conception or the belief that the soul is eternal."

Only you can decide what you believe deep down in your heart and soul. I just encourage you to think about it and ponder these deep but very meaningful and impactful questions. Did your soul live before you were born? Do you believe in a life after death or do you believe that once you take your last breath it is all over?

I feel the way you answer these two questions is very important to your long term mental wellbeing, and how you approach the trials that you face in this life. It is very comforting to me, to know that my spirit existed before being born on this earth, that there is a God and that I have a purpose here in this life and especially that there is life after this mortal life. And it is possible to be together as families, forever.

When you discover the answers for yourself, life will take on a new meaning and you will then be able to find true peace and happiness in your life.

ACTION ITEM: Ponder, meditate or pray and if you can, answer the questions – Where did I come from? Is there life after death?

SECRET #37 - PRACTICE THANKFULNESS

Think it, Feel it, Do it.

Did you know that adults and teens are not normally or naturally grateful? So to develop a *Thankfulness* or *Gratitude* attitude and have it a part of your life, it will require practice, daily practice.

Thankfulness comes in three stages:
1st   Recognition – Initial thought
2nd   Acknowledgement – Yes indeed, it is good
3rd   Appreciation – Better than the alternatives

Gratitude or Thankfulness is a thought process. This process might only take a second or two to run through the three stages. When you develop Thankfulness the process is done effortlessly.

According to research and studies, practicing Thankfulness has some very positive side effects, such as:

- Strengthens Relationships with family members and friends. According to a 2003 study, gratitude or thankfulness can boost pro-social behaviors, such as helping other people who have problems or lending emotional support to another person.
- Strengthens Mental Health in teenagers. Teens are happier, have a more positive outlook on life, and have more hope than those teens that do not practice Thankfulness.
- Better Sleep for those who took 15 minutes prior to going to bed and wrote down things they were thankful for.
- Improves Health including strengthening the immune system, and the heart. Studies showed that feelings of

appreciation and positive emotions slowed the heart rate and lowered the number of cases of sickness.

There are a number of ways to implement or increase Gratitude or Thankfulness in your daily life. Here are three ideas you can work on today.

1. Give at least one compliment every day. This can be a compliment to a person or you can ask someone to share your appreciation of something. (I appreciate _____, don't you?)
2. Make a promise with yourself not to criticize, gossip or complain for 7-10 day. If you slip up, that is OK, just start over. Take notice of all the energy you spend if a negative thought comes up.
3. Offer a Prayer of Thanks. In a 2007 poll 70% of those surveyed (all religions combined) said they pray daily. Studies show that those who say 'Thank You' more often than "please give me..." experience a higher level of satisfaction in life!

So now that you know about Thankfulness and how beneficial it is to your relationships, health (both physical and mental) and overall wellness, it is time to implement it into your daily life. When you are more thankful for the big AND little things in life the healthier and happier you will be.

ACTION ITEM: Everyday, share with another person, at least one compliment about something you are thankful for.

SECRET #38 - PRAYER

"Prayer is the key of the morning and the bolt of the evening."
— Mahatma Gandhi

A PRAYER is a *'solemn request for help or an expression of thanks that is addressed to God or an object of worship.'* It is also an *'earnest hope or wish'*.

Man has been praying since Adam and Eve and as long as man has been able to ponder his existence and life. For many people there is no established evidence that God or a Higher Power actually 'hears' your prayers but in recent years there is mounting evidence that prayer has measurable effects on your life and health.

Based on personal experience, I know that God hears and answers my prayers. Let's find out what the results are of some of the many research studies done on prayer and health. Prayer helps:

- Helps reduce stress – both physical and mental. Prayer balances out your emotional reaction to stress.
- Reduces your chance of suffering from anxiety and depression.
- Makes you nicer and reduces feelings of aggression.
- You become more forgiving.
- Increases your levels of dopamine, thus increasing your happiness level.
- Increase humility, less greedy for money and material things and just a better person.
- You live longer.

The results will depend on your expectations of receiving results. According to researchers from Baylor University, people who pray to a loving and protective God are less likely to experience anxiety-related disorders such as worry, fear, self-consciousness, social anxiety and obsessive compulsive behavior, compared to people who pray but don't really expect to receive any comfort or protection from God. So expect results and you will get results.

Prayer can be a mighty tool for healing, comfort and to boost your mood. Add daily prayer into your life and you will see wonderful changes in your health and happiness.

ACTION ITEM: If you do not pray, start by praying once a day for a week and see if you don't see and feel a difference in your life. If you do pray, try working on your 'expectations' and see if things improve.

SECRET #39 – MEDITATION

DEFINITION - *To Engage In Contemplation, Reflection Or Finding Deeper Meaning - To engage in mental exercise (as concentration on one's breathing or repetition of a mantra) for the purpose of reaching a heightened level of spiritual awareness or for relaxation.*

Meditation is different than Ponder. – Ponder implies figuring out a problem or making a decision. Meditate implies focused thought on something to find and understand its deeper meaning.

For thousands of years people in different cultures have used some form of meditation. Originally it was used to help people improve their understanding of sacred and mystical forces in life. In the modern Western cultures meditation is more commonly used to reduce stress by achieving a more relaxed state. But meditation is equally powerful in developing or increasing ones spirituality.

Since meditation is used primarily as a spiritual tool in the different countries where it originated, it has been put within the category of spirituality. The nice thing about meditation is that once implemented into your daily routine it will accomplish two major goals at once – stress management and spiritual growth.

Researchers at Harvard Medical School found that, those who did meditation daily over a longer time had far more active 'disease-fighting genes' compared to those who did not practice meditation.

Then the researchers ask the control group (who never did meditation) to start a daily meditation practice. 'After two months, their bodies began to change; the genes that help fight inflammation, kill diseased cells and protect the body from cancer all began to switch on.'

They also found that with regular meditation the positive and healthy effect kept increasing. In other words the more you practice meditation the greater your chances are of remaining free of disease and developing a stronger immune system.

Other laboratory studies have found that meditation produced positive changes in the brain circuits involving the regulation of emotions and the reduction of the stress hormone cortisol.

Meditation clears the 'monkey mind' and helps you be in the present moment and focus on just one thing. Meditation along with prayer can greatly influence and improve your spirituality while reducing your stress levels. Improve in both those areas and you will find more peace, harmony, health and happiness in your life. Meditate today!

ACTION ITEM: Try different types of meditation and find one you enjoy and do it daily for a week.

SECRET #40 - CREATE A GRATITUDE JOURNAL

Your gratitude journal does not have to be fancy or formal; it can be a simple notebook. It is up to you. What really matters is that you write in it on a regular basis – keep it where you can review it, especially on those down days.

So what do you put in a gratitude journal? Everything you are thankful for! Write down one or two things or experiences that you are grateful for and try not to duplicate any. You can list a couple of things that happened during the day that impressed you or what you learned from an experience.

Here are just a few reasons to start writing in a Gratitude Journal.

- o Improves your sleep – According to researchers if you spend 15 minutes before bedtime, writing and pondering things you are grateful for, you should fall asleep quicker, stay asleep longer and sleep deeper.
- o Improves attitude and may turn you into an optimist – Attitudes improve and you become more optimistic after writing in a gratitude journal and pondering over the list. Optimistic attitudes increase your overall physical, mental and emotional health.
- o The body feels every thought – Thinking about positive things and writing down things and experiences that you are thankful for helps the body and mind relive those positive moments.

- Letting Go of limiting beliefs – You are your own worst critic. You tend to see what you expect in life and those expectations are limited by your beliefs. If you can start to change those beliefs about yourself, your life will start to change.

Your future will thank you for it – In 10 to 20 years from now you will be a different person, **IF** you keep up a gratitude journal during that whole time. I think that you will feel healthier, happier, less stressed, more vibrant and just more fun to be around. Try to prove me wrong – keep writing in the gratitude journal for 10 years then look back and see if you are not a different and better person than when you started. I dare you!

ACTION ITEM: Start your Gratitude Journal. Write in it every night or at least once a week. Just list 1 or 2 things you are thankful for.

STRESS MANAGEMENT:

SECRET #41 - DEEP BREATHING EXERCISE

Did you know that breathing correctly is not only important for living longer but also in being in a good mood and performing at your best.

Deep breathing is a simple but powerful relaxation technique that focuses on full, deep and relaxed breaths. These deep breaths deliver the following benefits:

- A Quick Way To Reduce Stress And Anxiety Levels
- Elevates Moods And Reduces Depression
- Boosts Energy Levels And Improves Stamina
- Releases Toxins And Detoxifies The Body
- Relieves Aches And Pains
- Helps Strengthens The Immune System
- Simple And Very Easy To Learn
- Can Be Done Almost Anywhere
- The Cornerstone Of Many Other Relaxation Practices
- It Only Takes A Few Minutes And A Relaxing, Quiet Place.

There are many different techniques available. Most all deep breathing techniques use your abdomen muscles instead of your chest. Here is a simple basic deep breathing technique to help you get started.

EQUAL BREATHING

Step #1 -   INHALE through the nose for a count of four (4). Your stomach should rise. Balance within the body is a good thing and it all starts with the breath.

Step #2 -   EXHALE through the nose for a count of four (4). Your stomach should contract. This adds a slight, natural resistance to the breath.

Step #3 -   Repeat steps #1 and #2 for 2-5 minutes or until you are relaxed.

Breathing deeply from the abdomen is the key. This allows you to get more fresh air into your lungs. You inhale more oxygen when you take deep breaths using the abdomen instead of using your upper chest. You will feel less anxious and less tension when you are getting more oxygen into your system.

Deep Breathing can be done anywhere and anytime. The benefits are great and your moods and health will improve and energy levels will increase. Try it!

ACTION ITEM: Learn simple deep breathing techniques so when you need to de-stress or need a quick energy boost you can just start breathing!

SECRET #42 - YESTERDAY – TODAY – TOMORROW

"Yesterday is in the Past, Tomorrow may never come, Today is Now. Live Life Today."

Too many people live in the past. If you are always worried about what you did or did not do last week, last month or even last year you can easily develop anxiety issues or depression. You need to understand that yesterday is in the past and you can't live in the past all the time and stay emotionally and physically healthy. You can't change yesterday so learn from yesterday and make changes Today so you don't repeat the yesterdays.

Tomorrow never comes. Do you live in tomorrow? Do you wish your life away – 'I can't wait until Saturday'. Many people spend so much time worrying about tomorrow or another day in the future, that they miss out on Today. Again, if you spend much of your time thinking and worrying about tomorrow you will become discouraged, maybe depressed or suffer from anxiety. You need to plan for tomorrow but beyond setting goals or appointments don't worry about tomorrow.

Today is Now. Make the best of today because it will soon be gone and you can never get this time back. When these 24 hours are gone they are gone. This very moment should be the most important moment in your life. You need to make the most of it, not wasting time on trivial things such as gaming and texting.

Those people who seem to be able to focus on today, and make the most of it, seem to be less stressed, happier, healthier and more at peace.

ACTION ITEM: If there is something in the past that you worry about, then resolve it and move on! Enjoy the moments of today. Smell the smells around you. Embrace the warmth of the sun. Do what you need to do to BE in the moment and in Today. Tomorrow will take care of itself.

SECRET #43 - GUIDED VISUALIZATION

"What the mind of man can _conceive_ and _believe_, it can _achieve_"

Napoleon Hill

A guided visualization (or as some call it – guided imagery) usually consists of soft, beautiful and relaxing music with a male or female guide.

First the guide will gently talk you through a deep breathing exercise to get you relaxed.

Second, the guide will verbally take you to a wonderful, peaceful place. It could be a beach, in a forest or some place in the universe. The good ones will get you totally involved by describing the scene, - sounds, and smells getting you to use all your scenes.

Third, once you have arrived, the guide will give you positive statements or affirmations on whatever subject you are working on. OR they could have you visually preform a task.

Last, the guide will take you back to where you started your visualization journey. When you are finished you should be feeling relaxed and at peace.

The real power of guided visualizations or guided imagery is in the use of your imagination and visualization to train the brain and subconscious mind. Your subconscious mind then creates positive changes in your personal life. This is one of the main advantages of guided visualization and why they can be more powerful than passive, traditional meditations.

This type of meditation helps you to experience positive, vivid images in your mind that either directly or symbolically represent whatever changes you want to make in your life.

You are in such a deep state of relaxation, during a guided visualization, that the images your guide describes can become very vivid and alive. When you immerse yourself in a guided visualization session and you listen to the positive suggestions, it becomes a peaceful and powerful experience and the results are real and almost immediate. You will feel so much better, physically, emotionally, mentally and also spiritually.

> ***ACTION ITEM: Obtain a high quality Guided Visualization CD and use it every day for a week and see how you feel.***

Secret #44 - KIRTAN KRIYA (Saa Taa- Naa- Maa)

Kirtan Kriya – (KEER-tun, KREE-a) is a meditation from the Kundalini yoga tradition from India, and has been practiced for thousands of years. This meditation is sometimes called a singing exercise because it involves singing the sounds – Saa, Taa, Naa, Maa as you do a repetitive finger movement.

This is a non-religious practice and can be adapted to several lengths of time, but studies have shown that doing it *for just 12 minutes a day, reduce stress levels and increases brain activity in the area that controls memory.* Those who have memory problems, such as Alzheimer's disease, have found help performing this mediation daily.

How to practice Kirtan Kriya

1. While sitting with your spine straight and your eyes closed, and cross-legged (if you are flexible enough) repeat singing the Saa, Taa, Naa, Maa sounds. As you sing each sound, visualize the sound flowing in through the top of your head and out the middle of your forehead.
2. For the first two minutes, sing the sounds in your normal voice.
3. For the second two minutes, sing the sounds in a whisper.
4. For the next 4 minutes, sing the sounds silently to yourself.
5. Then reverse the order and whisper the sounds for two minutes and then out loud for the last two minutes.
   The total time: 12 minutes
6. To come out of or to finish the meditation, inhale very deeply, stretch your hands high above your head, and then bring them down slowly in a sweeping motion as you exhale.

The Finger movements (on both hands) while singing the sounds per the instructions above.

Saa – Touch thumbs to index fingers
Taa – Touch thumbs to middle fingers
Naa – Touch thumbs to ring fingers
Maa – Touch thumbs to little fingers

This is a very simple meditation after you have practiced it a couple of times. This is a great mental health exercise. Your body, mind and spirit will reward you for implementing Kirtan Kriya into your weekly schedule.

ACTION ITEM: Do a web search for Kirtan Kriya and find a video showing you how to do this meditation. Try Kirtan Kriya a couple of times a week and see if you can feel a difference after each session. If so, add it into you weekly routines.

SECRET #45 - DANCE THERAPY

Being a teenager is anything but easy. Between school, job, extracurricular activities and homework, it's hard to keep your mind focused while trying to be happy and relaxed at the same time. Being a teenager is a stressful time. But here is a new tip to help manage stress in your life AND help you learn and retain what you learn: **Dance!**

Your brain is still growing and developing and of course you want the strongest, healthiest brain possible, Right? Well sitting all day does not help produce strong healthy brains. BUT – Dancing does.

Here's the deal. Whenever your brain takes in new information or performs a new task new connections are being created in-between the neurons. Now when you add exercise, your body releases a protein in the brain that helps build and strengthens these new connections. This helps the brain to process, store and remember the new information better.

The Music Part

Part of the reason dance works so well depends on the music that you are dancing to. Most music can work well but before you go crank up your favorite music and start to gyrate your body all over the place, consider this. The best music is classical and slower, softer music. So the best type of dance is Ball Room, Ballet and Jazz. Break dancing may be great exercise but the music will counter the positive effects of the dancing. Consider the music before you go out and dance after you study or prior to taking a test. Save the rap and metal type of dancing until after the test.

Dancing can make you happier! Exercise produces hormones known as endorphins. These are the feel happy hormones. So dancing, any style may help improve well-being. Studies have shown that exercise (dance) releases a hormone that increases positive emotions and feelings which may help deal with depression.

Are you stressed out or suffer from anxiety. Dance can help. It can reduce muscle tension and stress which are leading causes of anxiety. Dancing helps eliminate or reduce brain chemicals that can cause stress and panic attacks. So if you feeling a little depressed or anxious do a little dancing and see if that doesn't help.

Actually dance has been used in therapy since the early 1900's. So if you are looking for more exercise or a nice 'do it yourself' therapy start taking a couple of dance classes. Dance will help put a smile on your face.

ACTION ITEM: Consider taking a dance class and learn a few specific dance steps. Find a few friends and teach them he dances and all of you will benefit.

SECRET #46 - MUSIC – CALMING AND HEALING

Music has always been an important part of every culture and society because of its healing powers and influence on the body, mind and spirit. There are some modern music that is detrimental to the mind, body and spirit. You know the music when you hear it. You start to feel your body tense up, heart rate increases and your head starts to pound. Choose your music wisely.

There are a lot of studies that show certain music has therapeutic traits. Let's take a look at some of them:

Pain Relief – Many studies have shown that if you listen to Classical music such as Mozart, Beethoven or Bach you can have relief from your muscle pain. Other calm, slow music has also been shown to help with pain. It only takes about 25 minutes a day for 10-14 days to help relieve back pain and as a side benefit – *helps you sleep better.*

Improved Memory – Research now shows that people who have memory loss respond best by listening to music of their choice (music from their childhood or early adult years). New research shows that memory was improved with those Alzheimer's patients who listened to music that they were very familiar with. Music can bring back memories from the past.

Control Your Heart Rate and Breathing – You can control your body, to a degree, simply by choosing the music that you listen to. A slow, meditative tempo has a relaxing effect on your body by slowing down your heart rate and breathing. Listening to faster music with an upbeat tempo speeds up your breathing and heart rate. So again pick your music wisely.

Increase Learning and Memorization – There have been hundreds of studies that have proven that just by listening to classical music like Bach, Beethoven and Mozart learning increases substantially. Memorization becomes much easier when done listening to a Mozart Concerto. So when you need to learn something quickly, play classical music when you study. You will be amazed at how quickly you will learn the material.

Your problems become easier – Music helps you to express your emotions. It is called 'Melodic Encouragement' which helps you to let go of suppressed feelings and emotions. Music can help you release those suppressed feelings. If you cry, that's OK. Tears represent feelings that must be expressed. As they say, 'Feeling is Healing.'

Soft, relaxing music has medicinal and learning properties and can elevate moods. Use music to relax and heal.

ACTION ITEM: This week listen to different soft classical or new age music and find several you like. Listen to them several times a week. Music soothes the savage beast within.

SECRET #47 - WRITE IT DOWN

What we are talking about is using a pen or pencil and a piece of paper. It seems that we are losing the art of writing. According to research the actual writing down of information helps to better retain that information. It is the physical act of writing that sends signals from your hand to your brain that builds motor memory. These motor memories are more easily retained and for longer periods of time.

Not only is writing beneficial for memory retention, it has many other health benefits such as:

Helps Improve Attitude During Stressful Times – In a 2008 study, Cancer patients were asked to do "Expressive Writing" (express their fears, hopes and dreams). The results found that this helped the cancer patients think about their disease in a different way, and it also improved their quality of life.

Improve Self-Love – Write a Love Letter To Yourself – As weird as this sounds, writing a love letter to yourself is a great way to feel better about yourself. Write a letter explaining all the good qualities you see in yourself. It is OK to pat yourself on the back once in a while. As we talked about earlier, you have to love yourself before you can truly love someone else.

Goals Are Easier To Achieve –The old adage; 'A goal not written is only a wish' is very true. Write down your goals – be specific and give them a time frame. Some goals can just be put on a 'bucket list' and forgotten – but somehow they still come to pass. There is just something about writing goals down. Do it!

Forgiveness Letters – You can write a letter forgiving yourself or someone else that has offended or hurt you. Just doing the act of writing it all down helps the forgiving process.

Writing down happy memories, things you are grateful for, your fears or goals will help you retain the memories, overcome fears and help your life be healthier and happier.

ACTION ITEM: This week spend more time writing down your thoughts and feelings, both happy and sad, both loving and forgiving. Don't forget about your goals and dreams.

SECRET #48 - LAUGHTER

Laughter can bring people together and improve relationships and over-all physical health as well as any medication or any other treatments out there. It also creates one of the best feelings during and after laughter.

Doctors and researchers have found that people who laugh a lot, tend to fight disease better than those people who do not laugh much and tend to be more negative. Laughter can increase your overall sense of well-being by having the following benefits:

Boost Immune System – Your T cells are immediately activated and begin to help you fight off sickness and disease. T cells are very specialized immune system cells that are just waiting in your body for activation. When you start to feel sick start to laugh and watch the cold or flu start to diminish.

Chronic Pain – Laughing helps your body to release endorphins, which can help ease chronic pain. Aching joints start to feel better during and after laughter.

Improves Mood – Laugh out loud if you want to lighten the mental load. Cortisol (stress hormone) levels are lowered in the body and also the levels of endorphins are increased, which help boost your mood. Research studies support laughter as a great way to break the downward spiral of depression.

Tones Up The Abs – Laughter can help you tone your abs. When you are laughing, the muscles in your stomach expand and contract, which is similar to when you intentionally exercise your abs. So add laughter to your daily exercise routine for firmer abs.

Laughter has shown benefits within the physical, mental, social, and spiritual areas of life. Therapeutic effectiveness of laughter can be derived from either spontaneous laughter (triggered by external stimuli or positive emotions) or self-induced laughter (triggered by oneself at will). Your brain is not able to distinguish between these two types. Benefits may be achieved either way. Laughter is Laughter, so just laugh!

ACTION ITEM: This week watch a funny movie, sitcom or read jokes, anything that will make you laugh out loud. See how you feel after.

PART 2 - SECONDARY FOODS

SECRET #49 - REPLACE THE BAD WITH GOOD – REPLACE THE GOOD WITH BETTER

This is a very easy *'first step'* in changing from the SAD – <u>S</u>tandard <u>A</u>merican <u>D</u>iet – to a healthier diet. You do not have to make major radical diet changes overnight. It can be done on a slower, more gradual pace. It is all about the journey, not perfection.

So the idea here is to take one unhealthy food from your diet and replace it with something better. You can do this once a week. Then you can replace the good items with something better.

Here is an example: Regular hamburger (bad – high saturated fat content) to Lean Hamburger (good – lower fat content). Then you can change from the good hamburger to Grass Fed Beef Hamburger (Better – low fat, no antibiotics and hormones, not gmo corn fed).

Fruit juices (bad) - whole fruit (good) – organic fruit (better/best). You get the idea!

You are what you eat so upgrade the quality of your food when you can. Start with getting rid of the highly processed foods, fast foods and soda drinks and go to whole foods then move on to organic where you can.

> *ACTION ITEM: Each week remove 1 unhealthy, highly processed food from your diet and replace it with a whole food, healthier version, and where possible go with organic. When it comes to meat go with grass fed.*

SECRET #50 - THE 90/10 DIET RULE

Changing diets for health reasons or for weight loss can be a daunting task. Many people think that when they *'go on a diet'* to lose weight that they must be perfect. They consider it a 'deprivation' diet. Weight loss is a journey not perfection. Changing from the Standard American Diet to a healthier diet does take some work.

Keep one thing in mind. It is OK to have a *'treat'* once in a while. Sometimes we slip up and eat that piece of cake, or have some of that 'white pasta' or slice of pizza. It is not the end of the weight loss journey.

Here is a good rule to base your diet on:

Eat Healthy 90% Of The Time –Treat Yourself 10%

This means that if you slip up once in a while it is not the end of the world. Here is the best part of this rule. IF you do really well on eating right all week then you can have that little splurge (couple of cookies, slice of pie, or whatever) on the weekend.

In other words, it is OK to slip up or have a little treat once a week, without wrecking your entire diet or feeling guilty. It will get easier with time. Experiment with different healthy dessert recipes until you find a couple that you like.

P.S. You don't need to be too fanatical with the healthy eating thing. This can be a turn off to family and friends. It is more important to stick to eating healthy, whole foods 90+% of the time than to stress out over eating perfect 100% of the time.

ACTION ITEM: This week try to eat healthy 90% of the time (whole foods) and when you do, give yourself a little reward. It is not about perfection, it's about the journey.

SECRET #51 - THE CROWDING OUT METHOD

One of the best solutions to overcome cravings and giving up your favorite unhealthy foods is by using the – **Crowding Out Method**.

The Crowding Out Method – Eat and Drink the foods that are good for you early in the day and you will leave less room for and minimize the desire for the unhealthy foods and drinks. Eating healthy foods first can and will crowd out the junk food.

Vegetables are high in vitamins and minerals. You can eat a lot of them without gaining weight. As you increase the amount of vegetables, in your diet such as dark leafy greens, your body will not have as much room for the processed junk foods. Here is the nice thing about this; your body will naturally start to crave these healthy foods.

This works well when it comes to hydration. In the morning fill a water bottle with water and take it with you and sip it steadily throughout your morning. Refill it for the afternoon. Do this and it will leave less room for coffee or soda and your body will respond better to the water.

The trick is to always have healthy foods and water available for snacks and especially when you are traveling. This will help you get through the day without impulsively eating junk food. This will take a little practice and planning, but it will be worth it. You will feel more energetic and happier. Crowding out the bad with the good works!!

ACTION ITEM: This week start increasing your intake of vegetables and water and see if you don't eat less processed junk food. Implement a 'Crowding Out.'

SECRET 52 - PURIFIED WATER – THE ELIXIR OF LIFE

If you research history you will find that the civilizations that developed and maintained the purest and cleanest water supply were generally the strongest, most vibrant and healthiest societies of their time.

Many of the ancient civilizations used water as part of their medical treatments to heal injury and to treat many different diseases. These included the Greek, Persian, Hebrew, Chinese and Native American, to name a few.

Maintaining the proper level of body hydration is an essential part of your biological functions. For example if the brain is not properly hydrated your thinking ability becomes impaired, you start having problems making good decisions, your grades suffer and your athletic abilities start to diminish. You increase your chances of getting headaches and dizziness. If your liver becomes dehydrated it cannot break down fats and you can start to gain weight and your digestive system becomes imbalanced, and so on.

So it is vitally important that you keep your body properly hydrated. Since studies have shown that most people are under hydrated, you need to increase the amount of water that you drink each day.

Caution: Chlorine and Fluoride - There is a huge debate on whether chlorine and fluoride should be added into the water supply. The debate also includes discussion about if Chlorine and Fluoride cause cancer or not. I recommend removing them from your water by using a high quality water filter system.

Two Rules of Thumb: Drink 8 - 8 oz glasses of water a day. Or ½ of your body weight in ounces. (weight = 150 lbs. 150 / 2 = 75 so drink 75 oz. of water)

Since each of you are different and unique, experiment with these two methods and see which works best for you. Your health will greatly improve just by making sure you get enough purified water into your body. ***Drink more water!***

> ***ACTION ITEM: Assess how much water you drink during an average day. Then increase that by 1-2 glasses and see how you feel.***

SECRET 53 - BE A COW NOT A CROC. – CHEW YOUR FOOD

Have you watched a cow eat while grazing in a pasture? How do they eat? They are always chewing. They chew, chew, chew, chew and chew some more – then they swallow. They are slow eaters.

Have you been to the zoo when Crocodiles are fed? So how do Croc's eat? You never see them chew their food. They chomp, chomp and swallow. They are fast eaters and practically swallow their food whole.

You should eat like a cow and not a croc! Some say chew 20 times and other say chew 50 times. You need to chew your food until it turns into liquid. Here are several reasons for chewing your foods more:

- Digestion actually starts with the chewing process. Digestion is improved with more chewing.
- Un-chewed foods can remain undigested and can cause bacteria overgrowth in the intestines.
- The chewing action and the production of saliva, sends a message to the stomach, intestines and to the whole gastrointestinal system that the digestion process has begun.
- The real flavors of plant foods are released only after they have been thoroughly chewed. This is also true with carbohydrates. The sweet flavors of these different foods become one of the rewards for eating and chewing.

Tip for chewing more –

- Put your fork or spoon down between bites. This slows down the eating process and allows for more time to chew.

I know that you have a busy schedule with school, part time jobs and maybe sport or hobbies, but you must slow down at meal time. For better health and elevated moods – chew your foods like a cow and not a croc!

ACTION ITEM: For each meal that you eat today, slow down, chew your food completely and really enjoy the eating experience.

SECRET 54 - IS SUGAR TOXIC?

The short answer is YES! Many, many studies have found a connection between sugar consumption and many diseases and weight gain. Here are some facts and reasons for you to start today removing added sugars from your diet.

Facts - 13% of the daily calories consumed by Americans come from **added** sugars in their foods. Based on this, you consume about 130 pounds of added sugar a year. That is equivalent to eating 22 teaspoons of added sugar a day! The American Heart Association said that the daily intake of added sugars for women must not exceed the equivalent of 6 teaspoons and for men they must not exceed 9.

Side Effects of exceeding these maximums:

- ✓ Causes the message "I AM FULL', that goes from your gut to your brain to misfire and causes your brain to think you are not full or that you have not eaten enough.
- ✓ Too much added sugar will irritate the lining of all your blood vessels which can impact the amount of oxygen that reaches all your different organs.
- ✓ When your liver receives an overdose of sugar, it has no choice but to turn the excess sugar into liver fat.
- ✓ Sugar triggers a Dopamine (a feel good neurotransmitter) response but when you eat too much sugar it starts to shut down the healthy signaling in the body. This means you have to eat more and more sugar in order to get that 'feel good feeling'.

Sugar is toxic to the body. All this added sugar to your food is slowly destroying your body. In order to live a long, healthy and happy life cut out most of the added sugars from your diet.

ACTION ITEM: Next time you go grocery shopping take time to read the food labels and only purchase foods with low sugar contents and without added sugars.

SECRET #55 - GLYCEMIC INDEX – EAT LOW GLYCEMIC FOODS

"Not All Carbohydrate Foods Are Equal"

The Glycemic Index (GI) is a comparative ranking of carbohydrate in foods based on how they affect blood glucose levels. Some carbohydrates are digested and turned into sugar (blood glucose) at a slower rate than other carbs. So a food with a GI of 30 will turn to sugar at a much slower rate than a food with a GI of 95.

"The glycemic index (GI) is a ranking of carbohydrates on a scale from 0 to 100 according to the extent to which they raise blood sugar levels after eating. Foods with a high GI are those which are rapidly digested and absorbed and result in marked fluctuations in blood sugar levels. Low-GI foods, by virtue of their slow digestion and absorption, produce gradual rises in blood sugar and insulin levels, and have proven benefits for health. Low GI diets have been shown to improve both glucose and lipid levels in people with diabetes (type 1 and type 2). They have benefits for weight control because they help control appetite and delay hunger. Low GI diets also reduce insulin levels and insulin resistance." Glycemicindex.com

Here is just a small sampling of foods with lower GI ratings and some with high GI ratings. Which foods are you eating?

LOWER GLYCEMIC FOODS	GI
Hummus (chickpea salad dip)	6
Grapefruit	25
Wheat Tortilla	30
Carrots (cooked)	35
Fettucini, average	32

HIGH GLYCEMIC FOODS	GI
Baked Russet Potato, average	111
Fruit Roll-ups	99
Bagel, White, Plain	95
Gatorade	78
Microwave popcorn, plain, average	55

http://www.the-gi-diet.org/lowgifoods/ is a partial list of foods and their GI rating.

ACTION ITEM: Look up some of the foods that you are currently eating and see how they rate on the Glycemic Food Index. Change foods if you need to.

SECRET #56 - EAT MEAT 'SPARINGLY'

Today there is a lot of debate on how much meat we should be eating, from being Vegetarian / Vegan to the other end, eating the Paleo / Atkins diets. I feel we should be somewhere in the middle. We should follow the 'sparingly' guidelines followed by some religious groups.

Several religious groups have a scriptural basis for eating meat 'sparingly', if at all. Two of the more prominent groups are the

Church of Jesus Christ of Latter-day Saints (The Word of Wisdom) and the Seventh Day Adventist. If you check the statistics they, as individual groups, have a much healthier and longer live span than other groups.

The definition of 'sparing' is left to each person's discretion. For me, I aim to get two-thirds of my protein from plants and just one-third from animal sources, or a 1:2 ratio. This is equivalent to three servings of meat (excluding two servings of fish/seafood) weekly.

A study done by Oxford University on the English diet, found that there was a reduction in the death rate from chronic diseases, when the meat intake was reduced to three servings a week. Three servings a week would be considered 'sparingly'. These researchers projected that this change in diet would have the following benefits for England:

- 331,000 fewer deaths a year from heart diseases
- 9,000 fewer cancer deaths a year
- 5,000 fewer stroke deaths a year

Environmental Food Toxins and Pollution

According to another study, it is estimated that nearly 85% of your toxin exposure from foods, comes into your body from the meat you eat. These toxins come in the form of hormones, antibiotics, GMO's that are found in the food fed to the beef. You can reduce your expose by doing two things – reduce your consumption of meat and implement Secret #57.

So reduce your risk by reducing your consumption of beef and other meats in your diet and use meat as a flavoring in cooking. Go ahead and implement this secret today for better health and happiness tomorrow.

ACTION ITEM: Decide what 'sparingly' means to you and try cutting your meat consumption down for a week or two and see how you feel.

SECRET #57 - MEAT – GRASS FED AND WILD CAUGHT

The Big Lie – *Meat is Meat is Meat* – It doesn't matter what the animal has been fed, the nutritional value is all the same. Here is the other part of the lie – The Hormones, anti-biotics and GMO foods given to the animals as feed are not harmful to humans.

Research is proving the lie is a lie. The difference between a grass-fed beef and a feed-lot fed beef is substantial. There is no comparison. Here are several advantages of grass-fed beef:
- Contains 1/3 to 1/2 the amount of bad fat which means it will lower your LDL levels
- Less Fats mean there are less calories
- Contains 2-6 times that amount of Omega-3 fatty acids
- Contains 4 times more vitamin E which helps reduce risk of cancer and heart disease

Free range Chickens produce eggs that contain as much as 20 times more Omega-3's than eggs from factory farms.

When it comes to fish and sea foods you want to only eat 'wild caught'. Much of the salmon sold in stores today come from fish farms. You have the same issues here as you do with the beef when it comes to anti-biotics and hormones. Now some farmed salmon are classified as GMO foods. There is always a concern for mercury in some seafood.

So when it comes to meat, go for quality. Go for 'Grass Feed', 'Wild Caught and Free Range' for your meat, fish and eggs. You will feel better and your moods may even soar.

ACTION ITEM: This week try eating some grass fed beef and cutting back on either the frequency or portion size of your meat and see how you feel.

SECRET #58 - BUY ORGANIC WHEN POSSIBLE

Go organic regardless of which diet you are on, even if you are on the SAD (Standard American Diet) plan. There is some debate on whether organic foods are worth the extra cost. You can make up your own mind. Here are several reasons why you will want to start adding in some organic foods into your diet.

- ♥ *More Nutrients* – Organics have more vitamins, minerals, micronutrients and enzymes than conventionally grown foods. Over 41 studies have shown the nutritional superiority of organically grown foods.
- ♥ *Reduce Chemical Toxins in the Body* – Did you know that there are currently over 600 different chemicals approved to use in commercially growing your foods? One study done by the National Academy of Science reported that 90% of these chemicals used have not been tested for long term health effects.
- ♥ *Avoid GMO foods* – To be labeled organic the food cannot be genetically modified. There is no mandatory GMO food labeling laws in the United States, so going with certified organic foods helps insure you are not eating GMO foods.

Again there have been little long-term health studies done on GMO's.

- ♥ ***Better Tasting*** - Organically grown heirloom varieties of fruits and vegetables just plainly taste better. This is because the soil is well balanced and this helps grow strong, healthy plants.

These are just a few of the many different reasons eating organically grown fruits, vegetables and meats are a better choice over commercially grown foods. When you make the change to organic you will feel physically and mentally better. Try it!

ACTION ITEM: Try the Organic version of a few different foods and help your body and mind feel better. Also try to educate your family on the benefits of organic foods.

SECRET #59 - THE CAFFEINE STRESS / DEPRESSION CONNECTION

Doctor Bruce McEwen said, ***"Stress, or being stressed out, leads to behaviors and patterns that in turn can lead to a chronic stress burden and increase the risk of major depression."***

Studies are now showing that when you drink and eat caffeine it really does induce a state of stress within your body. Caffeine causes the adrenal glands to produce stress hormones that can and will remain in your blood stream up to 18 hours after you consume it.

Drinking a cup of coffee can give you a shot of caffeine strong enough to increase stress hormones called catecholamines. The stress then turns on the switch to the 'fight or flight' hormone cortisol along with insulin. Insulin causes and increases inflammation within the body and this in return causes you and your body to feel lousy.

Stress that is caused by caffeine can produce the following:

- Mood Swings (Depression / Anxiety)
- Insomnia
- Muscle Tension
- Interferes with and weakens digestion
- Restricts the Blood flow to the Brain
- Accelerate Heart Rate and Blood Pressure

Sometimes the stress response switch fails to shut off, because of chronic stress, and it can lead to depression and all the other issues listed above. It is very important that this stress switch gets turned off.

The first thing you need to do is to cut back or eliminate caffeine from your diet – <u>soda drinks, energy drinks, coffee and some teas.</u> The *second* thing is to learn different techniques to help reduce and management all the other stress causing issues in your life.

ACTION ITEM: This week reduce the amount of caffeine in your diet and see if you feel less stressed.

SECRET #60 - WHOLE GRAINS - CEREAL

If you are not gluten intolerant and can tolerate grains, the question then becomes how much grain should you be eating?

According to a new study published in BMC Medicine, women who are eating about 1,800 calories should be eating about 53 grams of whole grains a day. For men it is slightly more.

When it comes to Cereal you must look for the word "Whole"_____. So when it comes to buying cereal the first ingredient should be 'whole-_____ flour.' Anything else means refined grains.

"When it comes to Whole Grain foods always follow this rule of thumb –

More Fiber than Sugar."

Here are some other helpful tips on finding healthy cereal.

1. FIBER – The more fiber the better. Do not settle for anything less than 3 grams per serving. The more fiber you can get in your cereal the longer you will feel full. Fiber is a must for healthy digestion and to keep you regular.
2. LIMIT SUGAR – Breakfast cereal is not a dessert! The low sugar in the cereal will help you avoid the sugar crash later on.
3. PROTEIN – Look for cereal with at least 5 grams of protein per serving. This will help you from overeating later. If your cereal meets all the other requirements but this one, just add an egg or yogurt to your meal.
4. READ THE INGREDIENT LIST – The first ingredient must be 'whole grain' and be limited to just a few ingredients, that you can pronounce and that sound like a food. Avoid highly processed foods.
5. PORTION SIZE – With cereal you may be tempted to eat more than one serving. Stick with the serving size for a few days and see how you feel. I think you will find that with

the healthier whole grain cereals you will not need to eat as much.

Feel free to 'bulk' up your cereal with some chopped nuts or a little fruit. Adding more Whole Grains into your diet will help you feel healthier and happier – IF you can tolerate the grains. Try adding more grains to your diet and see if you start to feel happier and healthier.

ACTION ITEM: When you go shopping with your parents this week search out and try a healthier 'whole grain' cereal. Also look for other ways to increase whole grains into your diet.

SECRET #61 - WHOLE GRAINS – BREAD

Just like with Whole Grain Cereals you need to look for those breads that have as the first ingredient – Whole wheat, whole rye, whole oats, etc. And like it was discussed in Secret #60 your bread must have more fiber than sugar. This seems like it would be easy find a lot of bread that meet this requirement, but it is not.

More Fiber than Sugar

With bread there is another ingredient that you must watch out for and that is Sodium or Salt! Try to stay under 200 mg per slice. We get enough salt in all our other foods so keep it down on the breads.

Here are the numbers for the bread that I buy from the local grocery store – Great Grains Bakery, Multigrain Flax Seeds & Omerga-3. It may not be the best on the market but it is affordable and the numbers look good:

Per Slice - serving
- Sodium – 170 mg
- Total Carbohydrates – 24 grams
- Dietary Fiber – 5 grams
- Sugars – 1 grams
- Protein – 5 grams

The sodium is low and there is more fiber and protein than most bread and the sugar is low. But like anything else, keep the consumption of the bread down even if it is healthy, moderation in all things.

If you have gluten intolerance then you will have to look for a healthy alternative.

ACTION ITEM: This week talk to your parents about upgrading the quality of your breads to more whole grains. Just make sure there is more fiber than sugar and it will be an improvement over the standard white bread.

SECRET #62 - VEGETABLES – 5-7 SERVINGS DAILY

I know there are exceptions but generally speaking kids and teens don't like vegetables. But it is essential for your overall wellbeing that you eat at a minimum of 5 servings of vegetables every day. 7 servings is better.

The serving sizes vary but as a general rule ½ cup of chopped, cooked or raw veggies is considered 1 serving. When it comes to raw leafy vegetables like a green salad, a serving is 1 cup. Since different vegetables contain different amounts and types of nutrients eat a variety.

As bare minimum, eat dark green leafy vegetables such as kale, spinach and beet greens several times a week.

These are really loaded with vitamins and minerals. These are easy to put into your diet. Just put them in a salad instead of, or in addition to, the iceberg lettuce.

Unless you are a vegetarian or vegan you probably are not in the habit of eating a lot of vegetables. So what will it take for you to get into the habit of eating 5-7 servings of vegetables each day? Here are a few tips.

   a. Constantly remind yourself to eat more veggies, even if you need to put post-it notes up.
   b. Have veggies available everywhere: home, school and eating out.
   c. Make it easy and quick for you. Prepare the veggies ahead of time.
   d. Start to add the veggies in slowly over a couple of weeks. This will allow your body to adjust. Veggies contain lots of fiber.

Here are a couple of ideas on how to get more vegetables into your daily diet.

   a. Talk to your parents and make sure they buy more veggies to keep around the house.
   b. Eat a dark leafy green salad most days and add in different veggies such as carrots, zucchini, broccoli and cucumbers to beef it up.

c. Have mom add some vegetables into some of your favorite dishes like zucchini into lasagna, broccoli spears into the mac and cheese or your quesadillas. You get the idea.

d. Have a good hearty vegetable soup once a week and a nice vegetable stew.

You will definitely notice a difference in your health and moods when you increase the amount of vegetables in your daily diet.

ACTION ITEM: This week increase the amount of veggies in your daily meals and see how you feel at the end of the week.

SECRET 63 - THE GREAT EXPERIMENT: Vegetable And Fruit Smoothies

Since the USDA's recommendation is 5-7 servings of vegetables and 2-3 servings of fruit a day, a great way to get this amount into your daily diet is through smoothies and especially green smoothies. There are hundreds if not thousands of green smoothie recipes available to you on the internet. (See the links below for some recipes)

Smoothies and Juices are NOT the same thing. Juicing takes everything out (pulp) except the juice. Smoothies use most of the whole fruit or vegetable. Smoothies are usually loaded with fiber and other nutrients found in the pulp. So I prefer smoothies over juices. Smoothies can be made in a blender. Juicing requires a special juicing machine.

If you are new to drinking smoothies here are a couple of beginner tips:

- In the beginning, use more fruit than dark leafy greens and other veggies.
- Over a few weeks, slowly add in more veggies and less fruit.
- Once your smoothies are a majority of veggies you can experiment with the 'other greens' like green algae chlorophyll, alfalfa sprouts, etc., as these have very strong flavors. Start with just a sprinkle and work up.
- You can try adding in protein powders or foods that are high in protein like chia seeds or ground flax seeds.
- Make sure you have a high quality blender. Cheap blenders may leave chunks and not make the drink smooth.

Again, experiment and see what works best for you. Try different recipes and find a few that you like the best and start using them in your daily or weekly meal plans. Get your mom to join with you; she will like the weight-loss benefit. I drink smoothies nearly every week day morning for breakfast and save the heavier breakfasts for the weekend.

ACTION ITEM: This week find two smoothie recipes and try them out. Then keep trying different recipes until you have 5-6 that you really like and add them into your daily diet.

Smoothie Recipes:
http://healthyblenderrecipes.com/recipes/raw_vegan_spicy_vegetable_green_smoothie

http://www.incrediblesmoothies.com/recipes/big-blend-fruit-vegetable-smoothie-recipe/

SECRET #64 - BERRIES IN SEASON – WHOLE FOODS – Rich In Antioxidants

Berries are special because they contain high levels of phytochemicals, which help protect cells from free radical damage. It is the damage by free radicals that cause aging, disease and many other physical problems with the body.

Eating berries has a huge impact on the brain and improves memory and helps elevate moods. According to research, berries contain 'Polyphenolics' which helps in the cleaning process in the brain and helps remove build-up of toxins from the brain. This helps the brain function properly and helps with memory retention. So eat some berries while doing homework.

In another study the researchers found that women who ate two servings of strawberries or one serving of blueberries a week showed less mental decline than those women who did not eat berries during the study. This is due to a group of compounds called 'Anthocyanidins'. These compounds are able to cross the blood-brain barrier and get in to the brain to work their magic.

These powerful antioxidants have a wide variety of positive effects on the brain and body. Pesticides and herbicides are routinely used in the production of berries and especially blueberries, so use organic berries when possible.

If you feel physically healthy you will be more inclined to feel mentally healthy.

ACTION ITEM: This week add a couple of servings of fresh berries into your meal plan. Blueberries are a wonderful addition to Buckwheat pancakes. Strawberries and Blackberries are great in smoothies.

SECRET #65 - HEALTHY SNACKS – Create A Daily Snack Plate

The idea here is to have your healthy snacks prepared in advance and easily available for when that 'Snack Attack' hits.

I can remember years ago, as a child, visiting my grandparent's farm and seeing a big bowl of fruit on the counter. If I was hungry, and it was not close to meal time, I knew I could just grab an apple or banana and eat it. It was quick, easy and I did not have to ask.

You can do the same thing but with a slight twist – Include some vegetables. Make a plate with fruit and veggies on it and set it out. Then whenever you (or a family member) are hungry you can just grab a carrot stick or slices of zucchini – you get the idea. You can also put some nuts and seeds on the plate also.

On school days you can have snack bags pre-prepared, full of fruit slices, veggies, nuts or seeds. You can just grab one and throw it in with your lunch and take it with you. If you don't have it with you at school you are going to run to the vending machine and buy junk food.

Nearly every morning I put my snack bags together. I have one small snack bag full of veggie slices, such as carrots, sweet potato, small sweet peppers and zucchini. The other snack bag is full of homemade granola or a mixture of dried fruit, nuts and seeds and I alternate throughout the week.

This is a simple idea; - prepare your healthy snacks ahead of time, so they are available when the need arises. It does not take long to put a healthy snack plate together and the rewards are great. You must feed your body healthy snacks if you want the brain to be healthy and to have a healthy and happy life.

ACTION ITEM: Every day this week make a healthy snack plate if you are going to be home. On school days take a healthy snack bag with you to enjoy.

SECRET #66 - VITAMIN L – LOVE In Home Cooking

One of the most potent vitamins found in some foods, one which can kill cancer cells, reduce pain and improve mental health is Vitamin L – LOVE!

Do you know which foods contain the most Vitamin L?   Answer: Most all Home Cooked Meals contain generous portions. Cooking meals at home is how the love gets in the food. If the food is 'home-grown' it even contains more Vitamin L.

Think back to last Thanksgiving dinner. Thanksgiving dinners seem to hold a lot of pleasant memories for many people. Think of the meal and how good it tasted. For most families, Thanksgiving dinners are all home cooked dishes. You can almost taste the love that everyone puts into the cooking of the meal.

Here is another example – I can remember how much better peanut--butter and jam sandwiches tasted when my mother made them for me. They always tasted better than the ones I made myself, even though I used the same peanut butter and jam. It was because my mother put some of her love into making the sandwich.

Vitamin L can be obtained from eating home cooked meals together, as a family, around the dinner table. Love and food have been known to be 'the glue' that holds families together. Traditions are born and preserved around the dinner table eating home cooked meals.

Try helping your mother cook the next meal. You can share a little of your love by helping with cooking. You can feed yourself a little – self-love.

ACTION ITEM: This week eat at home, around the table as a family, while enjoying meals cooked from scratch. Make sure you help with the preparation of the meal and put thought and love into the food while you help.

SECRET #67 - HEALTHY, TRADITIONAL FATS – Butter, Olive and Coconut Oils

"Eat Healthy Fats!"
"Eating Healthy Fats Does Not Make You Fat!"

You have been told to eat a 'low fat' diet. All the dietitians, doctors and such said that eating too much fat was bad for the heart and made you fat. Well in recent years, studies are showing that this is not necessarily true. It all depends on which types of fats you eat. There are some very healthy fats that you don't have to really worry about eating too much of.

You should be getting 20%-35% of your calories from healthy fats according to the 2010 Dietary Guideline for Americans. Just make sure that most of your fats come from the following sources…

Coconut Oil: This oil is loaded with medium-chain fatty acids. These are much easier for your body to digest and harder for the body to store as fat. Also these are broken down into smaller sizes so the cells can utilize the energy almost immediately. Coconut Oil is gaining a reputation for improving memory and brain functions.

Real Butter: Butter nearly became a casualty in the war on fat or the low-fat diet craze. Butter is now making a recovery since the health benefits of butter are becoming more widely accepted. Real Butter contains good healthy Omega-3 and Omega-6 which are known to help improve skin health and especially important for healthy brain functions.

Extra Virgin Olive Oil (EVOO): Several cultures have known about the health benefits of EVOO for centuries. All diets should include Olive Oil. This oil contains high amounts of antioxidants which protects all your cells from damage. As with the previous mentioned healthy oils, EVOO is great for memory and cognitive function plus it reduces inflammation.

Non-Traditional Sources of healthy fats

Avocado – These are one of the healthiest fruits you can eat because of the numerous health benefits. This delicious green treat is rich in monounsaturated fats, which lower the bad cholesterol while raising the good cholesterol. The Avocado is loaded with

Vitamin E and Vitamin E is great at preventing free radical damage and helps boost your immune system.

Don't forget that the Avocado is loaded with healthy protein and has more than any other fruit.

Omega-3 Fatty Acids: Since your body cannot produce Omega-3's you must rely on your diet or take a supplement to supply these nutrients. There are 3 different kinds or types of Ogema-3s: EPA – eicosapetaenoic acid, DHA – docosahexaenoic acid and ALA – alpha-linolenic acid. The one's you need to be the most concerned with is EPA and DHA. They are found in sea-foods like Salmon and Sardines. ALA is found in some plant foods, most notably, nuts and seeds and in high quality grass-fed beef.

Include Fats in your daily diet. Don't be afraid that you will gain a ton of weight because it just won't happen. I use lots of coconut oil in cooking my vegetables, put avocados in my smoothies and butter on my buckwheat pancakes. I am staying slim and trim and feel great. So can you.

ACTION ITEM: This week if possible start incorporating more healthy fats like Avocado, Coconut Oil and Olive Oil into your meals. Your brain, body and mood will thank you.

SECRET #68 - REFINED SEED AND VEGETABLE OILS – Cut and Reduce

There are good fats and bad fats. In secret #67 we talked about how to add healthy fats into your diet. Well now we are going to talk about the unhealthy fats that you need to remove from your diet.

Not all fats and oils are created equal. Many oils are unhealthy and hazardous to your health. These oils are highly processed and heated, cleaned with chemicals and use GMO corn, canola or soy. Do a google search and watch a couple of video's on how vegetable oil is made. It will change your mind about these cooking oils.

Here is a partial list of some of these oils that you should start to work on reducing from your diet and replacing with the healthy fats in #67.

- Vegetable Oil
- Soybean Oil
- Corn Oil
- Canola Oil
- Hydrogenated Oils
- Margarine
- Any oil that is labeled as refined, hydrogenated, partially-hydrogenated

These oils contain huge amounts of Polyunsaturated fatty acids called Omega-6, which can be harmful to your cells if you consume too much. If the ratio of Omega-6 to Omega-3 is too high it can be harmful to your body and mind. Your ratio needs to be in the 4:1 to 1:2 ranges. The average American diet has a ration as high as 16:1. This is why you need to either increase your Omega-3 fatty acids and/or reduce the Omega-6 fatty acids. The best plan of attack is to do both – reduce the Omega-6 and increase the Omega-3 in your daily diet.

These bad oils contribute to inflammation, loaded with trans fats, increase your risk of heart disease and ratio of Omega -6 to Omega

-3 has been shown to have a strong association with risk of severe depression.

So for better overall health and to lower your risk of depression work on getting as many of these highly processed oils out of your diet. Your body and mind will love you for it.

ACTION ITEM: To help improve you moods and overall health start to remove and replace these unhealthy oils with the healthy coconut oil, olive oil and avocados. Start reading the food labels and look for the fats.

SECRET #69 - MIDDAY SUNSHINE – VITAMIN D, The Missing Nutritional Link

As a teenager you probably do not have a deficiency in Vitamin D but you can never be too safe. Just know that you do not want to join that group. Be proactive!

It is estimated that more than 1 billion people worldwide are deficient in vitamin D. Why is this true? Answer: Humans are spending less time in the sun today than at any point in human history.

One of the most important preventive measures you can take to improve your overall health and happiness is to make sure you get sufficient amounts of Vitamin D. There are now hundreds of studies that link Vitamin D deficiency to higher risk of many different cancers, heart diseases, and mood disorders such as depression.

Signs of Deficiency:

1. You Feel Blue – Studies indicate that those with the lowest levels of vitamin D were 11 times more at risk to be depressed than those who received healthy daily doses.
2. Your Bones Ache / Soft Bones - Aches and Pains and Fatigue.
3. Cognitive impairment in older adults.
4. Increase death rate from cardiovascular disease.

The best source and the only natural source of Vitamin D is SUNLIGHT. When you get your Vitamin D from sunshine your body uses only what it needs and gets rid of the extra. If you are in the normal range you will need 1,000 – 2,000 IU a day to maintain good health.

Here is list of several good sources and quantities of Vitamin D you can expect to get from them.

Sunlight Exposure   10-15 minutes (arms and legs exposure v.s. most of the body exposed – Depending on where on the earth you are living)   3,000 – 20,000 IU

Salmon (3.5 oz. of fresh, wild caught)   600 - 1,000 IU
Salmon (3.5 oz. of fresh, farmed raised)   100 – 250 IU
Milk, Fortified (8 oz. glass) (milk has no natural Vitamin D) 100 IU

As you can see Sunshine is the best source, if you live where the sun is strong enough, and contains enough quantity of UVB rays to provide Vitamin D. So here is my recommendation, unless you live within a thousand miles from the Equator – go on a 15 minute walk around noon and take a Vitamin D supplement.

Get your daily dose of vitamin D – first from sunshine and second from foods and supplementation. Either way, make sure you are getting enough of this Sunshine Vitamin for a healthy mind, body and overall great health. So when you are feeling 'blue' increase your daytime walking.

ACTION ITEM: Don't rely on drinking a glass of milk for your dose of Vitamin D. Be proactive and increase your day time walking AND take a good quality Vitamin D supplement and watch your spirit soar.

SECRET #70 - FIRMENTED FOODS – Health Starts In The Gut

A healthy gut is the keystone to having a healthy body and mind. If you have a leaky gut (microscopic holes in the gut lining) or your gut bacteria are all out of balance, your body will feel lousy and your mind and moods can be way out of balance.

There are a lot of different nutritional therapies that can help improve your health but one that can really boost your overall health and wellness is adding fermented foods to your diet. Your gut needs help to heal and become healthy and eating different fermented foods is just the answer.

All the different fermented foods are just over-flowing with good bacteria or 'probiotics'. There are also countless research studies demonstrating how having a balance of good and bad bacteria in your gut forms the foundation for mental, emotional, physical and overall wellbeing.

Here are some benefits of eating traditional, fermented foods;

- *Loaded With Important Nutrients* – Some fermented foods are a great source of Vitamin K2. Just 15 grams of Natto daily provide all your daily K2 needs. B Vitamins are plentiful in fermented food.
- *Body Detoxification* – The beneficial bacteria are great detoxers (if this is a real word). They are capable of withdrawing a wide range of different heavy metals and toxins from the body.
- *Natural Source and Variety Of Microflora* – Supplements only contain a few different beneficial bacteria but eating a variety of fermented foods will add a much wider array of beneficial bacteria into your gut.
- *Boosting Your Immune System* – Did you know that your gut contains around 80% of your immune system? Probiotics and a healthy gut play a critical role in the development and the operation of the mucosal immune system in your digestive tract. And this aids in the production of antibodies to kill pathogens (viruses and germs).
- *Cost Effective* – Adding small amounts of good quality or homemade fermented foods to each of your meals will give you 100 times more probiotics than most supplements.

Here is a short list of fermented foods (buy at health food store when possible);
- Tempeh (fermented soybeans)
- Miso (fermented paste made from barley, rice or soybeans)
- Sauerkraut - Raw (fermented cabbage – easy to make at home)
- Yogurt (labeled – "Live & Active Cultures")
- Kefer (fermented milk drink – easy to make at home)
- Kombucha (fermented tea – can be made at home)
- Kimchi (Korean fermented cabbage)

o   Other Misc. Vegetables

You must have good gut health if you want to achieve a higher level of over-all wellness and improved moods. To obtain and maintain good gut health you need to add fermented foods to your daily diet or take a probiotic supplement. Check out the GAP diet if you have digestive issues. Probiotic foods are an important part of this diet. It is a great diet for Autism and most mood disorders.

ACTION ITEM: This week add some real, unpasteurized fermented foods into your daily diet. Go slow with small amounts and build up from there.

SECRET #71 - EGGS: Buy Quality – The Healthy Protein

Eggs are among some of the most nutritious foods as they contain a little bit of almost every nutrient your body needs to maintain wellness. The whole egg contains all the required nutrients to turn a single cell into a baby chicken.

Try to buy quality and purchase either Omega-3 enriched or pastured/free ranged eggs. These even contain a lot more Omega-3's and Vitamin A and E than the cheaper eggs. It is worth the investment.

A single egg is packed with 77 calories, **6 grams of high quality protein** and 5 grams of healthy fats. The quality of the protein is so high Eggs are used as the standard by which all other foods are measured. Remember Rocky Balboa (Sylvester Stallone) chugging down those drinks full of raw eggs as he trained for the big fight?

He needed the high quality protein to help build muscle, strength and endurance. (I don't recommend drinking raw eggs)

Eating a couple of eggs in the morning will give you enough fats and especially protein to keep you feeling full and give you the energy needed to keep going till lunch. Protein is needed throughout the day for good health.

Many people will not eat eggs out of fear that it will raise their blood cholesterol levels. It is true that eggs are high in cholesterol, BUT they do not affect blood cholesterol. The reason is – the liver actually produces large amounts of cholesterol every single day, so when you eat eggs, the liver just produces less cholesterol instead. So the cholesterol level remains consistent. Eating eggs will raise the "good" cholesterol (HDL) which is a good thing.

EXTRA BENEFIT - Eggs are a brain food! 1 whole egg contains 100 mg of CHOLINE. Several different dietary surveys show that nearly 90% of all the people in the U.S. are not getting the recommended daily amount of choline. In other words, most likely you are deficient in choline.

Choline is used to produce signaling molecules that are used in the brain. You may be wondering why your mind is not as sharp as it should be and why you may be suffering from depression, anxiety or some other mood disorder. It may be because you are deficient in Choline. Eat a couple of eggs and give your brain and mood a boost.

Eggs are healthy and they are not to be avoided unless of course you are on the vegan diet, or you have a known egg intolerance or allergy.

ACTION ITEM: This week try adding in a couple of extra eggs into your diet. If you already eat eggs on a regular basis, try upgrading the quality of the eggs and buy Free Range Eggs or at least the Omega-3 enriched eggs.

SECRET #72 - WHOLE GRAIN FLOURS - Use As Fresh As Possible

Nothing tastes better than fresh, homemade bread from freshly ground flour and other healthy ingredients. You will have to trust me when say this IF you have never had a slice of fresh, warm homemade bread. Let's not forget about the higher nutritional value of using fresh ingredients.

Whole grain flour loses most of it nutritional value within a few days of being ground. Also the wheat germ oil that is found in whole grain flour will start to turn rancid. So think about how long that whole grain flour has been sitting on the grocery store shelf before your parents end up buying it. This is one reason some flour smells a little rancid or moldy.

There is some testing that shows that within 72 hours of the milling or grinding process up to 90% of the nutritional value has been destroyed. Once most of the vitamin and minerals have been destroyed and the flour turns rancid the only thing left are some empty calories from the starch. When you eat starch it quickly turns to sugar which causes glucose spikes within the body.

If you buy freshly ground flour you will know that you are getting the most nutritional value possible. You will know that you are getting the whole grain and all the nutrients possible such as:

- Insoluble fiber,
- Magnesium
- Riboflavin
- Thiamine and Niacin
- Iron, Zinc
- Vitamins B1, B2, B3, E
- Polyunsaturated Fatty Acids

So when you start to cook and bake, use only the freshest whole grain flour possible. Either grind your own or find a bakery or other retail outlet that grinds whole grains daily. Whole grains are an excellent source for fiber and other important ingredients. Your body and brain will appreciate you and reward you with awesome health and a more stable mind.

> ***ACTION ITEM: This week find a bakery that makes and sells freshly made whole grain bread. Buy a loaf and see if that bread tastes better. Make a commitment now to only use fresh whole grain flour in all future baking.***

SECRET #73 - CHIA SEEDS – King of Energy, Omega-3 Fatty Acids, Protein and Fiber

I Love Chia Seeds! I put these little seeds in my drinking water, which makes the water alkaline. I put them in my 'overnight refrigerator oatmeal' that I eat as part of my lunch. I even add them to my buckwheat pancakes. These little seeds are chuck full of great nutritional stuff.

Chia seeds are a great source of Omega-3 Fatty Acids, Protein and Fiber. They are a great source of Magnesium, Manganese, and Phosphorus, providing about 1/3 of our daily requirements with just 2 tablespoons a day.

Here are few other reasons to add Chia Seeds to your daily diet:

- Weight Loss – due to the high protein and fiber weight loss can be enhanced with chia seeds
- Loaded with Antioxidants – Helps to destroy free radicals that cause diseases
- Loaded with important bone health nutrients like calcium and magnesium
- Improves Exercise Performance – The Ancient Aztec warriors ate chia seeds especially before battles.
- Very easy to incorporate into your diet. They are rather tasteless so you can add them to most dishes without disturbing the favor.
- Lower in real carbohydrates – Most of the carbs in Chia Seeds come in the form of insoluble fiber.

Again I just love Chia Seeds and I know you will too. Start by adding some Chia seeds to your bottled water (gently shake the bottle for a minute or two first to keep the seeds from forming a glob on the bottom) and you will notice a difference. Give your body the nutrients it needs to keep itself healthy.

ACTION ITEM: Purchase some Chia Seeds and start adding some to your water, sprinkle on yogurt or add some to your pancakes or other baked goods.

Secret #74 - DEEP FRIED FOODS – Know The Oil Used!

Before you eat any foods that are deep fried, find out what oil(s) were used! Many restaurants and fast food establishments cook their fried foods using man made oils that contain trans fats. These trans fats can be reused over and over again which helps keep the cost down for the establishment. Partially Hydrogenated Oils contains trans fats and is another name some people use instead of trans fats.

According to the American Heart Association – Trans Fats (partially hydrogenated oil) can 'lead to heart disease' in some people. The evidence is quite convincing. So much so that several European countries and Canada have either banned trans fats or severely restrict its use.

Many of these different vegetable oils and trans fats are created in an industrial chemical making process that adds hydrogen to a liquid vegetable oil to make them more solid when not heated. The main source for these trans fats are found in processed food with an ingredient called "partially hydrogenated oils".

Back in November of 2013, the FDA put out a statement that said partially hydrogenated oils were no longer classified as 'Generally Recognized As Safe' in foods for humans. The main reason companies put these fats into their processed foods is because it gives foods a desirable texture as well as flavor.

Here are 3 types of oils you should remove from your deep fried cooking.

1. Canola Oil – It comes from one of the top 3 GMO foods in the U.S. and is used by most all restaurants and fried foods in the grocery stores.

2. Corn Oil / Corn by-products - Again this is a GMO based oil and foods. The GMO contains pesticides to protect again bugs. When you eat this you potentially are putting these pesticides into your body.
3. Soy based Oils and Soy by-products – All soybeans are now GMO unless specified otherwise.

There is only a couple of ways that you can eliminate or reduce your exposure to trans fats. *One* - before you order your meal at a restaurant or a fast food establishment, ask which oil they use. *Two* - before buying fried foods look at the label to see what oil was used. Just by removing most fried foods from your diet will go a long way toward losing weight, and improving your overall health. Another healthy tip: Replace the trans fats in your diet with monounsaturated or polyunsaturated fats, these are the healthy types of fats.

ACTION ITEM: This week find out what oils are being use to cook your foods. Try to reduce the amount of fried food you eat, especially if it is cooked with Trans-fat oils.

Secret 75 - LIFE'S BEST HEALTH LESSON: Plant A Vegetable Garden

Gardening is one of my hobbies. It is a place where I can come home from work and relax as I plant, water and harvest. I have a couple of small fruit trees on one end of the garden space. I have blackberries, raspberries and my pride and joy – Goji berries. I have a Strawberry patch and 5-6 raised beds where I grow different types of squash, kale, tomatoes, beans, etc.

You may even have done some work in a garden in the past. You may have had a chore to weed the garden. So here is a question to think about – 'Why is having a garden important?' My answer may surprise you – "*It is the best health lesson*". I find peace and relaxation and for a little while the cares and worries of life are left outside of the garden. Everyone needs a place where they can do some deep thinking. Mine is while I am digging in the dirt, prepping the soil and watering. I think about my life – the good times, the trials and what I have learned from them.

I don't consider working in my garden work – well except on those hot July and August evenings when I have to water the garden. I just enjoy being outdoors and listening to the birds and a couple of chattering squirrels in the nearby trees. Another great reward is bringing in and eating the harvest.

You and your Family can have a similar experience by putting in a small garden in the corner of the back yard. Here is another advantage – you will eat more vegetables if you helped to plant, water and pick them. Home grown veggies and fruit are the healthiest foods you can eat.

Gardens provide some pretty good exercise also. Gardens teach you about 'The Law Of The Harvest' – you reap what you sow. Gardens will teach you reverence and greater appreciation for the food you eat especially when you help grow it.

Yes, there are many lessons on health that can be learned or accomplished by growing a garden. While your garden is growing you will learn some pretty important health lessons, if you will just take the time to look for them.

Even if you live in an apartment you can grow a few simple vegetables or herbs in potted containers. In some areas there are community gardens that you can get involved with and enjoy working together to grow food. Your spirits will soar as you put work and love into growing food.

ACTION ITEM: This week evaluate your situation and see if you can grow a small garden. If so plan it out and start working toward having a garden.

SECRET 76 - EAT A RAINBOW – Colors Of Fruits And Vegetables Matter!

Try eating all the different colors when it comes to fruits and vegetables. Think – red, dark green, yellow, white, orange, blue and purple. This will provide your dishes with eye appealing color but more importantly – a broad range of nutrients. So 'think variety, think color' and you can win the healthy nutrition game.

Make sure you are getting a wide variety of foods within each color. You must get a variety of foods in order to get all the needed vitamins, minerals and essential nutrients your body needs to be healthy and happy. This is especially true if you are a 'picky' eater.

The Color Key for Fruits and Vegetables:

Yellow and Orange – Vitamins C and A (Citrus Fruits, Squash)

Green – Vitamins K, B and E (Avocado, Kale, Spinach)

Purple – Vitamins C and K (Grapes, Eggplant, Red Cabbage)

You get the idea. The plants get their colors from the different phytochemicals found in them. It is these different phytochemicals or colors that offer the different nutrients when they are eaten.

When it comes to your overall health and mood enhancement, just remember that focusing on just one vitamin or nutrient is generally a bad idea. You will do more good by just eating a well-balanced and well-rounded diet and you will get most of the nutrients you need, in a form that your body will be able to use.

It might be a dumb saying – 'Eat the Rainbow' but it comes with a lot of wisdom and experience. So for your physical and mental health – "Eat The Rainbow" – add variety and color to your diet and your body and mind will be healthier and happier.

ACTION ITEM: This week eat some different fruits and vegetables that you may not have eaten before or in a long time. Add variety and color to your daily diet.

SECRET #77 - OLD FASHION VITAMINS – Whole Foods (Veggies, Fruit, Legumes, Nuts, Whole Grains And A Little Meat

How did your Great Grandparents get their daily dose of vitamins and minerals when they were growing up?

It was from one of two sources: Cod Liver Oil (if the family could afford it) and Whole Foods.

Getting your vitamins from Whole Foods is a new and fresh idea today. Growing up, your grandparents did not have all the supplement pills we have today. They had to get most everything from whole foods like – Veggies, Fruit, Legumes, Nuts, Whole Grains and a little Meat.

When I was little and went to visit my grandparents, do you know what I remember eating? I remember home cooked meals – home made everything. The soups were generally homemade, along with the bread. The meals always seemed to have a little of everything, veggies, beans, nuts, whole grains and some meat.

Today, the prevailing attitude is – Eat what you want and take a cheap 1 A-Day Vitamin and all is well. Our grandparents believed in eating nutritious whole food meals and then take a spoonful of good quality Cod Liver Oil just in case.

So for good health, a healthy mind and happiness, take a stroll down memory lane and return to your roots and have your mom cook some of your grandma's traditional whole food meals. It will warm your heart and soul, not to mention improves your mood. Get some of those important old fashion vitamins into your daily diet.

ACTION ITEM: Get a few of your grandparent's favorite recipes that were handed down and have your mom cook them this week. For an extra treat get their favorite stew or soup recipes.

SECRET #78 - SUPPLEMENTS: A Time And Place (Omega-3, Vitamin D and Probiotics)

The time and place is today. IF you are eating a well-balanced whole food diet you may not need to supplement your vitamin and mineral needs. Let's assume you are one of the few people who take your lifestyle diet serious, you still may need to take supplements in three key nutrients. I highly recommend supplements for these three key nutrients:

- **Omega-3 Fatty Acids – Fish Oils**. Why? Because you would have to eat a lot of wild caught salmon to get enough Omega-3's to counter-balance the excessive amounts of Omega-6's in the Standard American Diet. Too much Omega-6's cause inflammation. Omega-3's fight off inflammation in the body.
- **Vitamin D** – As you may know most people in the United State live way north of the Equator plus we seem to be too afraid to go outside in the sun. Being in the sunlight is the only natural way of getting vitamin D. Some people drink milk to get vitamin D but you would have to drink gallons of milk a day to get the amount your body needs.
- **Probiotics** – If you are not eating a well-balanced diet with sufficient amounts of different fiber you probably are going to develop gut issues. The other alternative is to eat different fermented foods like fresh non-cooked or pasteurized sauerkraut. Most people do not like nor eat much fermented foods. So to get or maintain a healthy gut you must be feeding the microbiome within the gut.

So at a minimum, if you are eating the standard diet of highly processed foods, you must supplement in those three areas. If you do, make sure that the supplements are high quality. If so you will feel a difference. Depression / anxiety symptoms can be caused by a poor diet and a deficiency in key vitamins and minerals. So if you want to have a healthy body and mind consider taking supplements in these three key areas.

ACTION ITEMS: IF you are not feeling well either mentally or physically talk to your parents about taking a high quality Vitamin D, Fish Oil and Probiotics supplements to your diet for 90 days and see how you feel. You will be pleasantly surprised with the results.

SECRET #79 - PROTEIN: Eat Twice As Much Plant Protein Than Animal Protein

There is a huge debate in the world of nutrition concerning eating meat and how much meat a person should eat. You need protein in order to build muscle, rebuild cells and just plain be healthy as you continue to grow and mature. Meat is not the only source of protein, unless you have gluten intolerance.

There are several reasons that you should get the bulk of your protein from plant sources. Each source of protein has its advantages and disadvantages.

- Meat Protein:
    - Advantage – Complete source of all amino acids including all essential amino acids. Rich source of zinc and Iron (easier to absorb by the body than Iron from plant-based foods.)
    - Disadvantage – Can contain higher levels of saturated fats and dietary cholesterol. Contains low levels of fiber. The body has a harder time getting rid of excess meat proteins. Unless your parents get organic meat / grass fed meat (can be hard to find

and expensive) you expose your body to anti-biotics, growth hormones, etc.

- Plant Protein:
    - Advantage – Lower intake of dietary cholesterol and unhealthy saturated fats. Easier to find Organic plant proteins than Organic meats. You have to eat a variety of plant proteins to get ALL non-essential amino acids – thus getting a wider range of other valuable vitamins and minerals. Eating plant protein will also give you lots of fiber (you get two great nutrients for eating one source). The body can get rid of extra plant protein easier than meat protein.
    - Disadvantage – Soy Protein contains isoflavones, which resembles the female hormone – Estrogen. Too much estrogen in some women causes weight gain and a host of other unwanted health issues. You have to eat a variety of plant protein to get all the essential proteins. (But I listed it as an advantage also.)

Because of the advantages and disadvantages listed above, I recommend eating twice as much plant based protein than meat protein. There is also one more overall advantage of eating more plant protein than meat protein – According to a 2010 review of numerous studies, an article was published in "Nutrition in Clinical Practice" stated that individuals following vegetarian type diets have <u>lower body mass indexes,</u> <u>lower blood cholesterol levels</u> and <u>lower blood pressure </u>than non-vegetarians.

Adapt this secret into your daily diet as best as you can and see if you don't feel better, have happier moods and overall sense of wellness.

ACTION ITEM: This next week or two try eating less meat and more plant based proteins, such as, Quinoa, Soy (Tofu, Tempeh), legumes and other whole grains.

SECRET #80 - KALE AND SWISS CHARD: Eat A Dark Leafy Green Salad Every Day

Have you heard the saying; *'A Large Dark Leafy Green Salad A Day Keeps The Doctors Away?'* You haven't!! Well it's true! Dark Leafy Greens are the king of the veggies and Kale just might be the greatest of them all.

Here is just a small list of the health benefits of Kale and some of the other dark leafy greens. Start now and avoid some of these health issues when you get older.

- o Vitamin K – Just one cup of raw kale or any of the other dark leafy greens will give you adequate amounts of vitamin K. Deficiency in Vitamin K can lead to kidney and artery calcification, weak bones and cardiovascular disease. More info on Vitamin K in tip #86.
- o Lowers Cholesterol – Kale and Mustard Greens lower cholesterol. Steamed seems to work better for this. The fiber in these greens combines with bile to remove cholesterol.
- o Prevents Eye Damage – Spinach, Kale, Swiss Chard along with a number of other dark leafy greens contains a lot of carotenoids, zeaxanthin and lutein. These nutrients help filter high-energy light that can cause eye damage.

- High Calcium – Mustard Greens contains 55 mg; Swiss Chard contains 54 mg; and Kale has 49 mg. The slightly bitter taste reflects the higher levels of calcium.
- Reduction In Risk For Colon Cancer – Kale, Cabbage, Broccoli and Mustard Greens helped reduce the risk of colon cancer in a 2011 study published in the Journal of the American Dietetic Association.

For better health, whip up and eat a Caesar salad, or any other dark leafy green salad, every day. So as you can see – 'A Salad A Day Can Keep The Doctors Away!"

HINT: Use a healthy Oil and Vinegar salad dressing instead of the unhealthy creamy type dressings.

ACTION ITEM: Every day this week, eat a big dark leafy green salad, with healthier Vinegar and Oil based salad dressing. This is not a salad made up of a lot of iceberg lettuce and a few shredded carrots. This is salad with kale, spinach, chard and a host of other dark leafy greens and veggies.

SECRET #81 - FASTING: The Monthly Detox

There is an age-old religious practice that has some real health benefits - Fasting. There is one faith in particular that has fasting as part of their regular religious practices. The Church of Jesus Christ of Latter-day Saints (Mormons) practice a 24 hour fast, usually on the first Sunday of each month. Their fast is going without food and water for 24 hours.

Some initial studies have shown that there are health benefits to fasting. One study showed a correlation between fasting and reduction in the risk of developing diabetes. Another study showed a lower rate of heart disease among those that practice regular fasting – at least once a month.

But one of the main benefits of doing a 24 hour fast is it gives the body and its organs, such as your digestive system a chance to rest. Fasting may not provide a significant time to detox but it gives the detoxing organs (liver and kidneys) a little rest. It also allows the body to burn up any extra glucose in the blood stream. Because of this, diabetics may not be able to fast for as long or may need to do a juice fast instead.

There are some health benefits of fasting but there are other benefits as well. Members of The Church of Jesus Christ of Latter-day Saints are encouraged to donate the value of the two meals that they missed as a 'fast offering' to help provide for those who may be less fortunate or poor. They also believe that there is a spiritual component also – bringing their spirit closer to God as they pray during this time – usually for someone else who is struggling in life. So while you give your body a time to rest, you can also be giving your spirit a chance to grow. Your body will feel rested and rejuvinated after the fast. Your mind will be a little less foggy.

ACTION ITEM: Try 'Fasting' one day this month by going without food and water. If you have medical conditions then drink some juice throughout the day.

SECRET #82 - DAIRY: Use It Sparingly

Did you know that up to 75% of the people of the world have intolerance to dairy? It is either due to the lactose or casein within the dairy products. 90% of African American's and 80% of the Asians are lactose intolerant. These numbers are the results of thousands of studies.

If you take the time to think about it you would come to realize that humans are the only species that deliberately drink the milk of another animal. Do you normally see a pig sucking on a cow or a puppy sucking on a sheep? You get the point. Is it natural or healthy in the long run? This is just something to think about.

So if this is true it should not be of any surprise to find out that your immune system may not recognize milk and its proteins (casein) and sugars (lactose) as friendly food.

Lactose Intolerance just means you do not have the ability to digest Lactose, which is a sugar in milk. Since there is a huge brain-gut connection, when the gut is irritated by a food it can send bad signals to the brain. In one study, subjects who had lactose intolerance showed a significantly higher score on the Beck depression inventory test, compared to those without the lactose intolerance. Other symptoms include-

- Gas and Bloating
- Loose Stools or Diarrhea
- Throwing Up or Nausea
- Depression Like Symptoms

Casein allergy or intolerance is when the body thinks this dairy protein is a foreign invader. This attack on the casein protein causes the body many different problems. This type of intolerance or allergy is harder to diagnose and takes longer for the symptoms to appear. These symptoms may be;

- Diarrhea or Chronic Constipation
- Foggy Brain or Tingly Fingers and hands
- Joint Pain or Symptoms of Depression / Anxiety

The symptom of these two dairy intolerances can be very similar but then again they can be very different. But the one thing they have in common is the cure or solution. The solution is to remove milk and other dairy products from your diet.

If you are suffering from depression, anxiety or other mood disorders try removing dairy from your diet or minimize the amount you eat. It might just be that simple to cure your mood swings. You might find other benefits as well, such as less mucus and stuffy noses, less ear infections, etc.

ACTION ITEM: For 10 days remove all dairy from your diet and see what symptoms disappear. After 10 days slowly add dairy back into your diet and see if you notice any difference. You might be surprised to see your moods improve while you are off the dairy.

SECRET #83 - QUINOA, KASHA BUCKWHEAT) AND OTHER WHOLE GRAINS

Eating whole grains is another area that is widely debated. The discussions all center on gluten and gluten intolerances. If you have sensitivity to gluten then by all means stay away from gluten containing grains. BUT if not then add healthy grains to your diet. They are packed with healthy nutrients that will feed the body and the brain. Here are a few grains/seeds that you might not have in your current diet that you might want to try. Some of these are gluten free.

QUINOA – (keen-wa)
- Gluten-Free
- Complete plant based Protein that includes all nine essential amino acids
- Contains high amounts of protein, fiber, magnesium, Iron and Omega-3 fatty acids
- Great replacement for pasta, rice or couscous which contain gluten

KASHA or BUCKWHEAT
- Gluten-Free
- High in minerals – magnesium, copper, manganese, phosphorus
- High Fiber contents
- Another good replacement for pasta or rice

SPELT
- The Nutrients are easily absorbed by the body because it is highly water soluble
- Is much easier to digest than wheat and other grains because of its fragile gluten and high fiber content
- Good grain for those with digestive issues such as irritable bowel syndrome (IBS)
- Helps reduce LDL cholesterol levels and overall cholesterol levels
- Excellent source of phytoestrogens and lignans

MILLET

- Provides the body and brain with Serotonin to help calm and level your moods
- Is Alkaline and Digests easily
- Is a prebiotic or a food for the good bacteria in your gut
- Helps with having regular bowel movements because it hydrates your colon

As you can see, these different grains (some are technically seeds but used as grains) have different health benefits. It is important to have variety in your diet so as to get the different nutrients your body needs. This is also true with grains/seeds, so eat a variety of these and notice how your body and mind feels. I think you will be pleasantly surprised.

ACTION ITEM: This week pick one or two of these grains/seeds and learn how to add them into your diet. You might have to go to a health food store to buy some of them. Your body and mind will thank you for it.

SECRET #84 - FAST FOODS – Eat The Healthiest Items – The Businesses Will Change

Only buy the healthy items on the menu. These fast food places will never change unless we as consumers demand that they change. You do that by voting with your dollars. Here is just one example of an unhealthy meal – The World Famous McDonalds Big Mac

Big Mac   550 Calories   (This is just for the Big Mac – no fries, drink or cookie)

Nutrition Facts

Serving Size 1 sandwich (216 g)

Calories – 550	**Calories from Fat** - 261
Total Fat - 29g	**Saturated Fat** - 10g
Cholesterol - 75mg	**Sodium** - 970mg
Potassium - 0mg	**Carbohydrates** - 46g
Dietary Fiber - 3g	**Sugars** - 9g
Protein - 25g	

Fast Food companies will not make many changes to their menus unless people stop buying these calorie loaded foods. So here is the fast food health tip of the day – Limit your fast food meals to 1 a week! Your mind, mood and body will really appreciate it and they will reward you for your restraint.

ACTION ITEM: Cut your intake of fast foods to just 1 meal a week and when you do buy, make the healthiest choice possible.

SECRET #85 - COLLECT HEALTHY TRADITIONAL FAMILY RECIPES

There is something special when you cook using recipes handed down from your mother or grandmother. Remember that dinner your grand-mother cooked on special occasions that you just loved. Get the recipe before it is too late. But make sure they are the healthy ones, try to stay away from the cookies, and cake recipes since you are now trying to eat healthier.

I read a blog post from a gentleman whose father used to make the best homemade bread that he just loved. After his father passed away they could not find his special bread recipe anywhere. They later found out he made it from memory. Oh how this gentleman wished he had gotten that recipe from his father before his passing. Don't you wait until it is too late, get with your mother, grandmother, aunt or uncle and get their special recipes.

When you collect and use the healthy "traditional family" recipes you will help preserve some of the family traditions. This is especially true if the recipes originated from the 'mother' country. Since I am of German/Swiss descent, I sure wish I had my great grandmother's recipe for sauerkraut instead of the one I got off the internet.

There are several different ways you can save these recipes. Some individuals will start a Recipe Journal, either in a binder or on the computer. You can write them on recipe cards and file them the old fashion way, in a recipe box. Again it does not matter how you collect them, just start collecting them.

Your heart will be filled with fond memories when you start to cook and use the old family recipes that you collect over time. Your body and mind will be nourished in several different ways.

ACTION ITEM: This week contact your grandmother and get at least 1 recipe of your favorite meal. Then get your mother to cook that meal. This will help start your collection of family traditional recipes.

SECRET #86 - VITAMIN K-2 – Kale, Collard Greens, Other Dark Leafy Greens

Vitamin K has three main components – K1, K2 and K3. Vitamin K1 has a big impact on proper blood clotting. Little is known about Vitamin K3. In this section I want to focus on Vitamin K2 which regulates when calcium ends up in the body. K2 plays a huge role in bone metabolism and there are a number of studies that suggest it helps prevent fractures and osteoporosis as you grow older.

People that are deficient in Vitamin K have a much higher risk of bone fractures. This is especially true with senior citizens and is one of the contributing factors in their having higher rates of broken hips. Vitamin K regulates Osteoclasts which regulate how much minerals are pulled from the bones. When the osteoclasts are allowed to run wild and unchecked, too much of the minerals are pulled from the bones and the bones become weak, brittle and bent.

The K2 form of vitamin K is made within the body from K1 by your gut flora and other microorganisms. Because of this, you need to eat enough foods containing adequate amounts of Vitamin K1. The

K1 form of Vitamin K is found in plant foods. This is required in order for green plants to conduct the photosynthesis process.

There is very little K2 that is found naturally in foods UNLESS they have been fermented or otherwise processed using bacteria or other microorganisms. So fermented foods, such as Tempeh and Miso contains substantial amounts of K2.

Where do you find large amounts of Vitamin K? Well you probably guessed it – Dark Leafy Greens, such as, Kale, Spinach, Watercress and Radicchio just to name a few. Kale has by far more vitamin K than any other food – giving you 6 times your daily requirement. So add Kale and Spinach to your daily diet to insure you have healthy bones.

ACTION ITEM: Here is another reason to add Kale and Spinach to your diet. This week try to have Kale in at least 4 meals. Add to salads, smoothies or mixed steamed vegetables.

SECRET #87 - BREAK-FAST! The Most Important Meal Of The Day

There is much debate about this important topic when it comes to adults. But when it comes to children and teenagers there is little debate. You must eat a healthy breakfast during the growing and developing years. There are plenty of research studies that support the long standing nutrition mantra 'breakfast is the most important meal of the day.'

If you are eating breakfast and feel crappy and your moods are in the dumps then try changing your breakfast to a healthier breakfast and see what happens. _Dump The Cold Cereal And Milk Breakfast!!_

Here are a few reasons why eating a <u>healthy, well balanced breakfast</u> will help improve your health and moods.

- It will provide you with plenty of energy for activities at school or play during the morning and helps prevent the mid-morning slump.
- You will have a jump start on getting enough vitamins, minerals and other important nutrients that your body needs every day.
- There is a tendency to overeat at the next meal, or you will munch on junk food to hold off hunger.
- Can cause or increase mid-morning cravings which can make losing weight more difficult.
- Eating one or two large meals can make you feel sluggish, tired and add to feelings of depression after the meal.

Tips on breakfast meals and preparation
- In a hurry - Smoothies are fairly quick and easy and very healthy. I make mine the night before for a quick 'grab and go' breakfast.
- Make an egg omelet with lots of your favorite veggies. To save time cut up the vegetables the night before.
- Try to include 2-3 different foods and include- A Protein, Vegetables, A Whole Grain and maybe you can add a little fruit.

You will be healthier, more efficient in most all you do and your moods will greatly improve by recharging your brain and body every morning. You recharge by eating a complete and healthy breakfast.

ACTION ITEM: Start eating a healthy breakfast every morning. Change from the junk cereal to Egg and Veggie Omelet and a slice of whole grain toast with real butter.

SECRET #88 - CANDY: Buy 1 Piece At A Time – Never Buy A Box Or Bag

This is a sweet and short little secret. On occasion, when you want to have a sweet little treat just buy 1 piece at a time. Do not buy a whole bag or box and take them home! Repeat – only buy 1 piece at a time. You know if you buy a whole bag or box of candy and take it home you will eat all of them. This also holds true with cookies, donuts etc.

ACTION ITEM: This week, IF you purchase any candy or other sweet treat, just buy 1 piece at a time and you will automatically cut down on your consumption of sugar.

SECRET #89 - CHIPS: Only On National Holidays Or When Scooping Up Healthy Salsa or Dip

Chips and Dips have gone together for 50 years. They are part of the foundation of the Standard American Diet (SAD) along with Hamburger, Hotdogs and French Fries. Chips and all variations are a highly processed factory food. And for some teenagers they seem to the main diet item.

All the different variation of chips is nothing more than the starchy portion of a vegetable or grain, fried in refined oils with added salt and flavoring. Some may be baked or popped and have sea salt sprinkled on them but they are all highly processed and do not contain much real nutritional value.

Here is a list of the nutritional value from a handful (28 grams) of chips. The different types of chips vary but they are generally about the same – Calories: 140, Oxidized Seed Oil: 6-10 grams, Refined Carbohydrates: 16-20 grams and a dose of salt, no vitamins or minerals.

These foods seem to be fairly inexpensive but in reality they are not. These different chips range from about $3 a pound to $6 a pound. The best buy is home cooked popcorn.

So here is the real tip. Make eating chips a national holiday treat and only eat them with a healthy, homemade salsa or dip.

> *ACTION ITEM: Cut out all the different type of chips from your daily diet and only eat them on National Holidays and only with a healthy dip or salsa.*

SECRET #90 - LEGUMES: 5-6 Days A Week

Legumes are seeds that split in half. Some of the more common edible legumes are beans, peas, lentils, peanuts and soybeans. These seeds are a great source of fiber and protein plus a wealth of other beneficial nutrients. Because legumes have the ability to pull nitrogen from the atmosphere, which is important part of making the different amino acids, they are among the best plant based protein sources.

Legumes are a great source of healthy fibers. These healthy fibers consist of soluble fibers and resistant starch. These fibers pass through the stomach and small intestines undigested until they get to the colon or large intestines. Here they become food for the friendly bacteria and microbiome that live there. You need a healthy gut and in order to have a healthy gut you must keep the friendly bacteria well fed and happy.

These soluble fibers and resistant starches will help keep you feeling full, which will reduce the amount of food you eat and can help you lose weight in the long run.

Another great reason to consume legumes is because they are very cheap. They are one of the best foods where you get the most nutritional value for your money.

Worth noting – If you currently have depression or anxiety AND you DO NOT eat legumes then try adding them into your diet. You just might see the depression improve. But if you currently are suffering from depression and you have a fair amount of Legumes in your daily diet, try removing Legumes from your diet and see if your depression symptoms lessen. Some research suggests people who have intolerance to beans and legumes also have depression. Experiment with Legumes.

Bottom line – most people need to include properly prepared, legumes 5-6 times a week as part of a well-balanced, real food diet. You will start to feel healthier and happier in no time.

ACTION ITEM: This week add legumes into 3 meals. Try several different varieties and start off with smaller portions and then gradually increase frequency.

SECRET #91 - FRUIT: In Season And As Fresh As Possible. Frozen Work!

When it comes to eating fruit, keep these two things in mind – Eat the fruit as fresh as possible when they are in season. The next best thing is frozen fruit. Frozen fruit may be more preferable in some cases. Frozen fruit is ripe when picked and then quickly frozen. Most nutrients are still there in large quantities.

Fruit you purchase in the stores, if not in season, have been picked earlier and put in storage to be sold in stores later. These do not have near the amount of nutrients as those picked and eaten fresh. So eat fruit in season, fresh or frozen.

Since fruit come from plants, they are REAL, WHOLE foods. They are not highly processed junk foods. We have been eating fruit for thousands of years. Some people consider fruits as 'nature's fast food' because you can just grab and go. There is very little preparation time and some come in their own package.

Here is a short list of reason you want to eat 2-3 servings of fruit each day:

- Very Filling or Satiating – Because of all the fiber, water content and all the chewing you feel full and actually will eat less of the other foods. Look for fruit with the highest fiber, vitamins and minerals and with less sugar and calories.

- High in Vitamins and Minerals - such as Vitamin C, Potassium and Folate. Many people are deficient in Folate and Potassium. Let's not forget all the other various antioxidants and phytonutrients found in fruits.
- Natural Fructose – Yes fruit has fructose but it is found in small quantities and it is easily tolerated because it takes more chewing to eat the fruit and is slower to digest.

Because different fruits contain different nutrients and amounts make sure you eat a variety of fruits. Try a different fruit each week. Don't be afraid of some of the more exotic ones. Here is a list of a few of the top fruits based on nutritional content:

Berries – Blueberries, Raspberries, Strawberries, Blackberries, Gooseberries (Goji), Cranberries
Watermelon, Lemons, Grapefruit, Guavas
Higher in sugar – Apples, Banana's, Pineapples, Cherries, Mango and Oranges

Remember to eat 2-3 servings of fruit every day. Get them as fresh as possible and remember frozen fruit is good, especially in smoothies.

ACTION ITEM: This week try several different fruits, especially berries. Berries top the list of some of the most nutritious fruits.

SECRET #92 - SEEDS And NUTS - Variety: Eat A Handful Every Day

Nuts and seeds are very nutritious and tasty. More and more research shows that seeds and nuts help balance your moods and give your brain a powerful boost. So if you want to think clearer and/or give your moods a boost then munch on nuts and seeds when you study or do homework. Eat a variety and just a handful or so a day is all you need.

They all seem to help your nervous system to become healthier, which means you feel happier and your thinking is clearer. According to a Reader's Digest article "Fight Back With Foods" the under-consumption or deficiency in Omega-3 fatty acids can lead some people into depression. Your brain and central nervous system needs the following nutrients to function properly – Omega-3's, Vitamin E, Vitamin B6, Magnesium, Tryptophan, Phosphatidyl-choline and Choline.

They all seem to work well in clearing up 'brain fog' and feeling happier and healthier. Let's take a quick look at some of the seeds and nuts and find out why they help your brain and moods.

> **Walnuts:** They are an excellent source of nutrients for your brain. They contain a good amount of the Vitamins E and B6. Their contents are 15 to 20 percent Protein. They contain Linoleic Acid (Omega-6 fatty acids) and Alpha-linoleic acids (Omega-3 fatty acids).

> **Cashew Nuts:** These nuts are high in magnesium which helps to open up blood vessels in the brain which allows more oxygen-rich blood to flow to and through the brain.

> **Almonds:** They are an excellent source of Phenylalanine which is vital for proper brain function and neurological health.

> **Pecans and Peanuts:** Both of these nuts provide the brain with Choline, another vital nutrient for the brain. It is needed in ample amounts for healthy brain development and proper memory functions.

Flax Seeds: These little seeds are a great source of the mood-boosting Omega-3 fatty acids. These are a great replacement for those who do not like eating fish.

Pumpkin Seeds: High in Tryptophan. Eating a handful a day is a safe and natural way to reduce mild insomnia and depression.

Sunflower Seeds: Also high in tryptophan along with thiamine (a vitamin b) both are great for cognitive function and improved memory.

One of the most important nutrients for the brain, a major structural and functional component of the brain-cell membrane is Phosphatidyl-choline. If you are depleted in this, your brain cells will start to degenerate and die. Your body needs choline and lecithin to produce Phosphatidyl-choline. You need choline to produce acetylcholine which is a major player in maintaining good memory.

The good news is that nuts contain a good supply of choline and lecithin so your body can produce Phosphatidyl-choline and Acetylcholine for a healthy brain and good memory. Eat a handful of nuts daily and also eat a variety of nuts. Hundreds of studies have been done to support this secret.

Note: Tree nuts are on the Food Intolerance List because some people have intolerance to tree nuts or peanuts. If you suffer from a mood disorder and have no clear reason and you eat nuts on a regular basis, try to remove them from your diet and see if the depression symptoms clear up.

ACTION ITEMS: Include a handful of nuts in your daily diet and also include a variety, unless of course you have a known allergy or intolerance for peanuts and tree nuts.

SECRET #93 - HEALTHY DESSERTS:
Minimize Sugar – Use Winter Fruits

As a teenager I know you love a nice dessert after dinner. The problem is most desserts contain tons of added sugar. So here is a great tip – trade those highly processed, sugar laden desserts in for those with less sugar and use more Winter Fruits.

Fruit is considered nature's candy. Most are sweet and great tasting. Leave a bowl of fresh fruit and a bowl of fresh vegetables on a table and see which bowl is taken from the most. It will always be the fruit.

According to most lists out there the following fruits will be listed as winter fruits –

> Apples – most varieties
> Bananas
> Citrus Fruit – grapefruit, tangelos, clementine and all varieties of oranges
> Grapes
> Kiwi
> Pears
> Lemons

Here are a few dessert ideas using winter fruits, keep the added sugars to a minimum –

> *Apple Crisp topped with homemade Granola* – there are a lot of recipes available for both the apple crisp and the granola.

> *Fruit dipped in Dark Chocolate or melted Cacao* – Winter Strawberries need to be dressed up a little and chocolate

works great for that. Here is a great little video on how to dress strawberries in chocolate.
http://www.marthastewart.com/313844/chocolate-covered-strawberries

Baked Apple – Apples are plentiful and delicious. Baking an apple is simple, easy and tasty. Here is a popular recipe - http://simplyrecipes.com/recipes/baked_apples/

Tropical Fruit Delight – Mix chunks of ripe pineapple with slices of banana with grated coconut. Feel free to add in other tropical fruit like sliced kiwi.

Banana Nut Bread – There are tons of recipes available. Here are a couple of tips to make a healthier version of the bread. Replace ½ of the white flour with whole wheat flour or other whole grain flour. Cut the sugar by 1/3 and use brown sugar instead of the white sugar and use real butter instead of the less healthy oils normally called out in recipes. Don't forget to double the amount of walnuts.

Bottom line: In the winter, when you have that strong craving for a dessert after dinner, please think fruit and make it the main ingredient. When you make healthier choices your body, mind and moods will feel healthier and more alive.

ACTION ITEM: This week, reach for a piece of fruit or fruit filled dish when you want to help satisfy the 'after dinner dessert' craving.

SECRET #94 - SUPPLEMENTS – Amino Acids – Food For Moods

When it comes to brain health and happiness Amino Acids are one of the key nutrients. There are other important nutrients but amino acids are a major key in regulating moods. If you are suffering from symptoms of depression or anxiety, chances are really high that you are deficient in one or more amino acids. Let's take a quick peak at why this is the case. This might be a little technical.

Neurotransmitter molecules carry neural impulses around inside each of your brain's nerve cells. There are dozens of different kinds of neurotransmitters, each with their own important function. I just want to touch on 3 of these neurotransmitters:

Dopamine
Norepinephrine
Serotonin

These three are part of a class of chemicals called monoamines. These monoamines are critical in maintaining normal moods. They come into play in our experiences regarding fear and pleasure. Researchers also believe that many of your cognitive functions, like learning, memory and attention (concentration) are influenced by these monoamines.

Depression, ADHD, and Anxiety can be caused by the imbalance or disruption of these neurotransmitters. It is vitally important that you minimize these disruptions or deficiencies of these neurotransmitters by providing your body the needed associated Amino Acids. Let's take a quick look at which amino acids affect these neurotransmitters. Again this is a little technical but important to know and understand.

The body takes the amino acids that are found in your protein foods and converts them into the monoamine neurotransmitters. For example:

Phenylalanine is the amino acid that is converted into **Dopamine**

Tyrosine is needed to make **Noreprinephrine** (Noradrenaline)

Tryptophan is the amino acid that is needed to be converted into **5-HTP** which is converted into **Serotonin**. Tryptophan (found in food – not available as a supplement) is converted into 5-HTP (not found in food – is available as a supplement) is converted into Serotonin.

As you can see it is very important to get enough of all the different amino acids for a healthy brain and to overcome depression, anxiety and other mood disorders. Normally you can get enough of all the different amino-acids **IF** you are eating a healthy, well-balanced diet.

According to researchers, nutrition is one of the major contributors to your health and well-being including proper brain functions and moods. Many of the food patterns you experience during depression are the same ones that precede depression and other mood disorders. These include skipping meals, craving and eating sweet sugary foods, poor appetite and poor food choices.

Just like other important nutrients such as minerals, vitamins, and omega-3 it is a good idea to supplement your diet with Amino Acids. Researchers and Clinicians have found that taking an Amino Acid supplement have reduced symptoms of depression and help elevate moods. Researchers are doing more and more studies in the area of epigenetics (DNA-Gene expression) using amino acid supplements to help control different mood and brain disorders. The findings are very promising.

If you want a healthy brain and a happier disposition try taking an Amino Acid supplement. In the meantime try up grading your diet also. You will be glad you did.

ACTION ITEM: This week try taking an Amino Acid supplement and see if you can feel a little less stressed, calmer and happier.

SECRET #95 - Learn To Cook A Few Healthy Meals

Why would this be listed as one of the top 101 Secrets to Health and Happiness? Well it's very simple. In order to eat healthy you have to know how to cook healthy foods. You need great recipes, experience working with different kitchen appliances, etc.

Talk to your mom, other family members or even a neighbor about teaching you how to cook healthy meals from a recipe. Cooking from scratch is becoming a lost art. Society is accustomed to dumping food from a box and adding water and cooking it. This does not take much skill to learn. It is also not very healthy for you.

Consider taking a cooking class in high school, if they offer it. Check to see if there are any cooking clubs in your area that you can join. There are You-Tube videos that are available online.

It is important that you learn how to cook and especially how to cook from scratch following a healthy recipe. You are never too young to start learning. Again talk to your mom about teaching you to cook some of her favorite healthy foods. One day you will be leaving the nest and you will need to know these skills.

ACTION ITEM: Find a cooking coach and start learning the art of healthy cooking from scratch following a recipe. Learn to cook a few good healthy meals.

SECRET #96: - NIGHTSHADE VEGETABLES – Healthy For You, Maybe

Nightshade fruits and vegetables are nutritious and beneficial for most people. However, there are some people who have a sensitivity or intolerance with this group of foods, and are unable to fully digest them. Sensitivity may cause you to have symptoms of bloating, gas, nausea, and diarrhea. They can cause pain in the joints, headaches and symptoms of depression.

If you are suffering from any of the symptoms listed above you might try removing all nightshade foods from your diet for 30 days to see how you feel. If the symptoms clear-up then you know you have to avoid all nightshade foods.

Which foods fall into the nightshade category?

Potatoes – We are talking about white, red, blue-skinned and yellow varieties. Know that Sweet potatoes and Yams are NOT nightshade foods.

Tomatoes – This includes all tomatoes varieties, raw and cooked and this includes foods made from tomatoes, like ketchup, sauces and pastes.

Peppers – Bell Peppers, Cayenne Peppers, Jalapenos and Paprika to name a few. This would include any spice made from peppers such as Paprika and dried peppers.

Eggplants – These are fairly easy to avoid. Eggplants are used in various ethnic dishes such as Thai, Indian, and Italian. Eggplant Parmesan is one of the more well-known dishes.

Goji Berries – Since these are not all that common in our western diet, they are fairly easy to avoid. But these nutritious little berries are becoming more common in juices, smoothies and different nutritional supplements, so read the labels carefully.

Again, these foods are delicious and very nutritious for most people. Just be aware that if you suffer from depression, joint pains, or from digestive issues nightshade foods might be the cause and it is worth eliminating them from diet and then seeing how you feel.

If you find that you are NOT sensitive to nightshade foods make sure you try to incorporate them into your daily or weekly diet as they do contain a great amount of healthy vitamins, minerals and other nutrients.

ACTION ITEM: Experiment with nightshade fruits and vegetables. If you are eating them and your health is not where you want it to be try removing them from your diet and see if you look and feel better.

If you are not eating nightshade foods and feel like you need a boost, add them to your diet and see if you feel better.

SECRET #97 - STOCK-BASED VEGETABLE SOUPS - Homemade - Once A Week

Vegetable broths are a very healthy and versatile part of any diet. These broths are delicious, contain tons of minerals and will help alkalize your body and keep it from getting too acidic. Both vegetable and bone broths have been part of the human diet for thousands of years.

Broths and soups have been used almost as a medicine. Ask your grandma what she gave your mom or dad when they got a cold. I will bet your answer was she gave them chicken noodle soup or a vegetable broth. Vegetable broths are commonly incorporated into different cleanses or detoxes. Broths are used to heal the gut.

The tasty vegetable broths warms, soothes and nourishes the body. It has healing properties and help with;

- Boosting the immune system
- Brain health
- Joint pain and overall joint health
- Digestion issues
- Over all skin and body health

Vegetable broth can be used straight and sipped like a tea or as a base for soups or sauces. It is great to use in place of water when cooking quinoa, rice and kasha (buckwheat). It adds more flavor as well as additional nutrition.

Vegetable broth can be made from most any vegetables, but if you want to make a broth that has a deep flavor and immune boosting properties add the following vegetables to the pot:

- Shitake mushrooms or any other mushrooms

- Garlic
- Ginger
- Turmeric
- Kombu or any other seaweed

For a wonderful and nutritious vegetable soup stock recipe check out this one and give it to your mom and help her make a batch:

http://gourmandeinthekitchen.com/2014/detox-vegetable-broth-recipe/

Now that you have a recipe and some knowledge go ahead and make a batch of vegetable stock. Your mom can use it to make any dish that calls for soup stock. You can also make great vegetable soups using this vegetable stock as the base. Vegetable soups are really healthy and nutritious. Soups help soothe the body, mind and spirit. Try having a bowl full of vegetable soup or broth on a weekly basis and your body and mind will feel wonderful. It will also help keep the common cold away.

ACTION ITEM: This week help your mom make a simple vegetable soup stock. Then drink it like a tea and your mom can use it to cook with to add additional flavor to your dishes.

SECRET #98 - HERBS AND SPICES: Use For Flavoring And Healing

"Studies show that many different herbs and spices offer health benefits," so says David Heber, Director of the UCLA Center for Human Nutrition.

"We're now starting to see a scientific basis for why people have been using spices medicinally for thousands of years," says Bharat Aggarwal, Ph.D., professor at the University Of Texas M.D. Anderson Cancer Center in Houston.

Not only do herbs and spices add flavor to your food dishes but they also have many health and healing properties. Because of this it is important to your overall health to include many different herbs and spices in your food preparations. Let's take a look of at a few herbs and spices and their health benefits.

Sage: Sipping on sage tea is great for upset stomachs and sore throats. Studies have shown that spraying sore throats with a sage solution (sage tea) gives effective pain relief.

Chili Peppers: According to studies, the pungent compound in hot chilies – Capsaicin, helps to increase the body's metabolism and helps boost fat burning.

Ginger: Helps soothe an upset stomach, nausea, fights common colds and reduces arthritis pain. Throughout history ginger has been used in treating stomach troubles.

Rosemary: In a recent study individuals achieved higher scores on memory and alertness tests after piping in a mist of aromatic rosemary oil into their study rooms. Rosemary garlands were used by the ancient Greek scholars when they studied to help them remember.

Cinnamon: The ancient Romans, Greeks and King Solomon highly prized cinnamon and used it to relieve stomach problems and to boost appetite. Today it is used to stabilize blood sugar levels of Type 2 diabetics.

Parsley: This herb contains anti-cancer properties. Researchers at the University of Missouri have shown that parsley can actually prevent breast cancer-cell growth.

Turmeric: Turmeric is made into a paste and then it is applied to wounds to speed up healing, in India. They also treat the common cold and other respiratory problems with a turmeric tea.

Saffron: In Persian traditional medicine, saffron is used to uplift moods, and is made into a medicinal tea. They also use saffron in the preparation of rice dishes. Saffron has been used to relieve symptoms of PMS.

These are just a few of the very healthy and tasty herbs and spices. As spices, they all can help transform a dull and tasteless food into a very delicious dish. The great side effect of cooking with spices is it just may improve your health, mood and memory. Start adding spices into your daily food dishes. Don't forget to make and drink herbal teas when you are not feeling well.

ACTION ITEM: This week explain to mom about spices and help her experiment with different herbs and spices when cooking.

SECRET #99 - SUPER FOODS FROM AROUND THE WORLD

There are many different foods that have been used not only by ancient civilizations but also in modern times that are extremely healthy and beneficial but are not well known or used much here in the United States.

If you have a chance to add some of these foods into your daily and weekly diet you will notice a profound difference in how you feel. Since it is very difficult to get these foods fresh here in the United States they are usually consumed as a powder or dried. Let's take a quick look at several of these healthy superfoods from around the world.

Acai Berry - This can be easily found as a juice. Acai juice is super high in Anthocyanin, which researchers at Texas A&M, say will greatly increase the blood antioxidant levels because it is a powerful antioxidant.

Goji Berries – For hundreds and even thousands of years Goji Berries have been used in Chinese herbal medicine and is commonly used in herbal tea and tonic drinks. These tasty berries are a great source of Vitamin C and especially beta-carotene. They also contain 13% protein and are high in iron which helps to build up the blood. Goji berries also help to keep the liver and kidneys healthy and in shape and great for those who are anemic and need extra iron.

I just love adding a few of these healthy dried berries into my homemade trail mix, and refrigerator oatmeal. I even have a few plants in my garden.

Cacao or Dark Dark Chocolate - In the ancient America's, the Incas considered a drink made from cacao as 'the drink of the gods'. Cacao is available as a powder for making drinks and smoothies or as 'nibs' (chunks of roasted cacao) which are a crunchy treat.

Cacao contains Anandamide which is a mood improver and is known as the 'bliss' molecule. It helps create a feeling of euphoria. In other words it helps balance mood swings. It does this by helping to boost brain levels of the neurotransmitter – Serotonin, the feel good brain hormone. Studies have shown that cacao boosts the brain levels of calming hormones and helps restore a sense of well-being and happiness.

Maca – is a tuber (large radish like) that is grown at the higher elevation of the South American Andes Mountains. This plant has been used for centuries as an adaptogen (it helps anywhere within the body where it is needed).

It is critically important, especially in this stress filled world that we all live in, that you include a food like Maca into your diet. It is known to increase the body's resistance to fatigue, stress factors, anxiety and trauma.

Camu Camu – this Amazon fruit is known for its extremely high Vitamin C and antioxidant that is responsible for boosting immune system, neutralizing the damaging effects of those pesky free radicals and preventing oxidative stress in the body.

The Vitamin C in Camu Camu is powerful, natural and better utilized by the body than the Ascorbic Acid used in many vitamin supplements. Because of this, the Camu Camu Vitamin C, according to researchers, is one of the best nutrients for the brain, the central nervous system, skin and eyes and very useful in making certain neurotransmitters needed for ideal brain function. A healthy brain = healthy moods.

As you can see, there are some foods from other areas of the world that have some tremendous health benefits that you can try. These are found at most health food stores and online. Experiment with some of these tasty super foods from around the world and see for yourself why they have been used for hundreds and even thousands of years by the Chinese and the ancient people of South America.

ACTION ITEM: This week go to your local health food store and buy some Maca, Cacao or dried Goji berries. Add to smoothies or trail mix. Research and experiment with these amazing foods.

SECRET #100 - BONE BROTH – The Other Elixir Of Life

There are many people who consider bone broth as –"The Other Elixir of Life or Second Elixir of Life" behind water. Bone Broth can be used in place of water when cooking or just sipped as a tea. Either way, bone broth is very nutritious, healthy and delicious.

Bone broths have the following health benefits;

- High in Calcium, Magnesium and Phosphorus – great for building healthy and strong bones and teeth
  - Women who drink bone broth have babies with stronger and healthier bones
- High in Collagen
  - Helps remove wrinkles and cellulite
  - Lubricates the joints and helps with joint pain
  - Heals leaky gut problems and aids in digestion
- High In Amino Acid Glycerin
  - Supports better sleep
  - Aids the liver in detoxifying your body

How to make bone broth

Bone broth is made by boiling bones from healthy animals. This process pulls out the minerals, collagen and glycerin from the bones. Bones can be from beef, bison, fish, lamb and poultry, which ever ones you like to eat.

Steps to make bone broth
1. Blanch Bones – Boil bones for 20 minutes
2. Roast Bones – Roast at 450 degrees. Roast until the point of being 'too done'
3. Using a larger pot than you think you will need, add bones, little garlic, onion and black pepper and cover with lots of water
4. Simmer – Up to 24 hours for best flavor (unless using poultry then a few hours will due)
5. Strain out solids and Cool Quickly – add Ice and put in fridge.

There are a lot of recipes on the internet but for the best results keep ingredients to a minimum. Try bone broth and enjoy the health benefits that it can provide.

ACTION ITEM: This week help your mom make a batch of homemade bone broth or pick some up at your local health food store. Homemade always tastes better and you know what you are getting.

SECRET #101 - SULFUR – The Forgotten Mineral

Before you go wrinkling up or pinching your nose, I am not talking about the yellow stinky mineral that is mined or found in smelly sulfur springs. I am talking about the other Sulfur – the organic version that humans are absolutely dependent on for a healthy body and mind.

This sulfur is formally called MethylSulfonyMethane or more commonly called MSM. The term Organic Sulfur and MSM is the same thing and are commonly used interchangeably. Organic Sulfur is known for some pretty amazing health benefits. MSM is a critical mineral that is needed by every cell in your body. Organic Sulfur is needed for over 140 functions or to make compounds needed in your body. It is the 3rd most plentiful mineral in your body.

When was the last time you heard any doctor talk about Sulfur and the need to get enough of this mineral into your body? Very few people are talking about sulfur but they should be!

There are only 2 ways to get sulfur – Supplements and Foods. The problem is - in today's food there is very little sulfur, even in the sulfur rich foods. So the best way to get the sulfur you need is through supplementation.

Reasons why you should be taking organic sulfur –

- sulfur enables the transport of oxygen across cell membranes so the cells can regenerate efficiently
- Reduces joint inflammation and pain
- Supports the creation of insulin – reduces the need for insulin for diabetics
- Heals skin issues and promotes healthy and young looking skin
- Transports nutrients into the cells
- Needed in liver and cell regeneration
- The list goes on and on................

Because most of us have an organic sulfur deficiency, we all have health issues. People who take the organic sulfur report improvements in nearly every area of the body. Allergies go away, cataracts disappear, skin issues clear up, muscle and joint pains are gone, and on and on. It almost looks like a miracle supplement. My wife's coworkers comment on how good her face looks and how much younger see looks. They want to know her secret.

Organic Sulfur is the forgotten mineral but I strongly suggest that if you have some health issues you might just want to try taking MSM supplementation for 90 days and see if you don't feel better. It has no side effects and it is difficult to take too much. Try it and see what happens.

ACTION ITEM: This week try taking Organic Sulfur (MSM) supplement. For the best results take it in either Crystal or powdered form, mixed in warm, filtered water. Remember – it may not taste great but it is great for the body.

THE SUMMARY

As you finish reading this book I sincerely hope that you have found these tips helpful and enlightening. None of these tips were deep secrets from some far away Tibetan Monk or a book from some recently discovered civilization. They are simple everyday things you can do in your daily life.

I can promise you that if you will take these tips serious _**and implement them into your life**_, by doing the action items; your life will become healthier, happier and more peaceful. I realize that as a teenager living at home you will have to work with your parents to implement some of these action items. But as you share these tips with them they will see the wisdom behind them and will want to implement them into their lives as well.

You have learned that there are **Primary Foods** and **Secondary Foods** and that each of them play an important role in your health and happiness. You have learned that you cannot neglect either.

Neglect the Primary Foods and your stress level will go off the charts. Having great relationships with your parents, siblings, friends, school mates, and co-workers is a must if you are to obtain and maintain great health and have happiness in life. Having great relationships will come in handy when you do have some of those re-occurring down days.

Exercising and being active can, for some people, be the main thing that eliminates depression, reduce stress and increase happiness. Being active and exercising can be just as effective as medications. So get up and get moving!

The ideal situation is to be in a career or job that you love. This may not apply to you today but it will before you know it. Now is the time to start to find and understand what you love to do and what career paths you might find fun and enjoyable.

Let's not forget about Spirituality. Hopefully you will take time to think about your spirituality and what spirituality means to you. Once you know, do something every day to feed that spirituality. Having this in your life will help you overcome and deal with trials that will come up in your life.

As you may well know, STRESS KILLS! There are some great tips here on how to manage and deal with stress. Try some of the deep breathing exercises, learn some Qi Gong movements or implement guided visualization into your daily or weekly routine. Try to eliminate some of the sources of stress. Regardless of how successful you are at removing stress from your life, you must learn how to manage and deal with your stress. Life is full of stress so the sooner you learn how to manage it the better.

Now let's review some of the tips concerning the Secondary Foods. For many people the sources of their depression or anxiety symptoms may be from food intolerance or sensitivity. For this group of individuals finding out which foods, such as dairy or gluten, that they are intolerant of and removing them from their diet is all they have to do and the symptoms disappear.

Your brain needs all the nutrients it can get so chew your food well. Digestion starts in the mouth and the more you chew your food the easier and more complete the digestion is when it hits the stomach. Eating home cooked meals with your family is something that is becoming lost in our society. Use healthy foods as the glue that holds the family together to help strengthen family relationships.

You now have 101 great ideas on becoming a healthier and happier person but you have to take the first step and keep taking steps thereafter. These are easy, little steps, not giant leaps out of your comfort zone. It all begins with the first step and taking the next step – no matter what! You can do it - because I believe in YOU!

FAVOR: *If you found this book helpful and useful please go to Amazon and leave a 5 star review. This will help get this book in front of more teenagers. Also tell a friend about this book.*

RESOURCES:

Here is couple of resources that are available to you. Feel free to check them out and use them as you see fit.

DEPRESSION TO HAPPINESS –The 100 Day Challenge
Creator – Timothy Baumann, CHC

This is a 100 day challenge that will change your entire life IF you are ready and willing to put forth the needed effort. In the book and challenge we go into more details on many of the tips contained within this book. It includes 14 weekly emails with action items – similar to the ones in this book. The Challenge contains a complete 14 day detox, an elimination diet (to look for and find food intolerances) and a complete 28 day clean eating plan and recipes plus much more.

This is for those who are serious about regaining their health and/or overcoming depression, anxiety or other mood disorders.

There are two options within this 100 day challenge. You can choose between The DIY (Do It Yourself) version and the Group Coaching version. The Group Coaching is for those who want and need more support and encouragement.

For more information –
www.depressiontohappiness.com/the100daychallenge

The Happiness Journey 365

Full 365 Days or The 30 Day Challenge (trial)

Live Life One Day At A Time With Daily Thoughts, Exercises, Challenges, Recipes, Lifestyle Tips, Affirmations and Facebook engagement activities.

Here is how it works!

Every day you will receive an e-mail with something that will help you improve your health and happiness. For complete details and to sign up go to:
http://depressiontohappiness.com/thehappinessjourney365

Qsciences – EMPowerplus Q96 and other supplements

These are the supplements that my wife and I take. They have 20 years of history and over 34 independent studies done by top universities and researchers around the world. Specifically formulated and designed for the brain. The company also has most all the great supplements discussed in this book.

Information: www.brainsupplementsite.com Or
www.14166.myqsciences.com/products.aspx

BOOKS

NUTRIENT POWER – Heal Your Biochemistry and Heal Your Brain by William J Walsh, PhD

SUPPORT

This is a closed Facebook group that is open for those who have purchased this book and for those who participate in the 100 Day Challenge listed above.

https://www.facebook.com/groups/depressiontohappiness/

LIFE: PRIMARY WHEEL

HEALTH: SECONDARY WHEEL

Made in the USA
Middletown, DE
10 November 2019

78351279R00110